Y0-BZK-574

Courage and Resistance: Remembering the Warsaw Ghetto Uprising

BARBARA STEINER

AuthorHouse™
1663 Liberty Drive, Suite 200
Bloomington, IN 47403
www.authorhouse.com
Phone: 1-800-839-8640

AuthorHouse™ UK Ltd.
500 Avebury Boulevard
Central Milton Keynes, MK9 2BE
www.authorhouse.co.uk
Phone: 08001974150

First published by AuthorHouse. 3/8/2006

ISBN: 1-4259-2025-X (sc)

Printed in the United States of America
Bloomington, Indiana

This book is printed on acid-free paper.

Cover Art: Drawing by Peggy Lipshutz

Book Design: www.danielgraphics.com

Dedicated to Arnold, our children and our grandchildren

Throughout this book, the author follows the traditional, respectful Jewish way of referring to G-d by omitting the vowel.

*How do I say thank you to the people
who are my friends and
who made this book possible —*

*To Dalya Horvitz, who kindly encouraged me
and spent hours listening to my story and typing it;*

*To Kenan Heise, who fulfilled
his determined promise it would be published;*

*To Bob Ford and Marjorie Kriz, who generously
edited the manuscript;*

*To Peggy Lipshutz, whose illustration
adds so much to the cover;*

*And to Rich Cahan, who helped
make it a better book —*

*To all of them, I say todah rabah
and G-d bless you.*

CONTENTS

Setting the Scene

I am a survivor. I am a witness. Each of us needs to tell our story to all who will read or listen.

A fate that I will never understand chose me to survive.

From 1941 to 1945, the vast majority of the city's 350,000 Jewish residents—including all the members of my immediate family—had died from the terrible conditions there, had been capriciously murdered or were shipped off to death or concentration camps.

Only a handful of us—who were penned up on April 19, 1943 in Warsaw's ghetto—are alive today. That day was Passover, the celebration of the Jewish survival under the Egyptian pharaoh. The next day would be Hitler's birthday.

Heinrich Himmler had decided on a birthday present to the fuehrer. He would organize the mass murder of the perhaps 50,000 or less Jews were left in the Warsaw Ghetto in a three-day effort starting April 19.

Himmler's Gestapo-led troops entered the ghetto with tanks to carry out their task. They met not lambs led to the slaughter but a resistance to the death from some of the residents. They had smuggled in weapons or created them out of whatever they could find.

I was there as a witness and a participant.

I can never forget—nor should any of us—either the people who died or the heroes who rose and fought against the Nazis with determination and courage from April 19 to May 16. They are all part of the story, a destiny, determined for me to testify to.

First, though, I must say something about the Holocaust itself and how it is perceived or rather misperceived today.

I sat in the darkened room with my eyes covered, crying. The lecturer on the Holocaust was showing slide after slide of dead, emaciated bodies. I asked her afterwards, "Why did you do that? People need to understand, but they can do so without having to be overwhelmed with these kind of pictures."

My extended family living in Poland at the beginning of the war included 50 people. Many, if not most, are included in this record I make. I alone survived. I cannot forget them. We cannot forget what happened to the Jews and others victims of the Holocaust. History begs us to remember; but we also need to restore their individuality, humanity and dignity as best we can. Those photos of them as victims say little of their dignity, their courage, and their goodness. These people were alive. This is what I want told.

This is my story and that of those whom I knew and loved. My children and their children will never get to meet them, to hear their voices and to look up to their grandparents, aunts and uncles, cousins, and the companions of my childhood. I survived, but actually it was a different Barbara who did. It was not the soft person who I am today. Nor was it the sweet, pampered child who I was before the war.

The woman who once worked for our family when I was nine years old hit her baby. When the child cried, I did also, almost uncontrollably. One day when a man called me ugly names in the street, I ran home sobbing. My father told me, "This man says such things to those around him. You can get angry, but do not go that man's level and let it hurt you."

Such was the Barbara Zyskind, who at the age of 14 was living in Warsaw, Poland when the Nazis invaded and ruthlessly moved forward in their plans to degrade and destroy all of us, adult and child alike, who were Jews.

Still, this is the story of all three of us Barbaras—pampered child, hounded teenager and mindful woman—as well as of my family and the community in which I lived.

It is about those whose lives I shared and to whose deaths I can attest.

It is about the Jewish Warsaw Ghetto and the uprising in which we—men, women and children—fought the Nazis with every means we could.

It is about my father, who—though dead—found ways to help me survive.

It is about my future husband, who—by being willing to sacrifice his own life—extended mine.

It is about friends, especially other teenage girls my own age, who did not survive; but who have since shared my life by living on as part of my heart.

It is also about the inhumanity and the wanton cruelty and viciousness of the Nazis and those who, in any way, helped them.

It is about the Polish people, whose hostile and greedy voices I heard in the cattle cars that took us to the death camps as well as those brave ones who found ways to care even under impossible conditions and to resist when doing so meant certain and immediate death.

It is about urging people today to become part of the story by telling themselves and resolving, "Never again."

It is about the unshakable sadness that I carry with me, because it all really did happen.

PART I

Before the War

CHAPTER 1

Our Jewish Life in Prewar Poland

*...when I was a young girl, in spite of the rampant
anti-Semitism throughout Poland, I experienced
Jewish life as alive and vital and thriving in Warsaw.*

Warsaw was where I was born as had been both my father and mother and their families. The city, as I remember it, was beautiful. It had large, expansive avenues, lush parks, lovely theatres and fine museums. I remember well the ornate, exquisite opera house where I saw several performances as a child. There was the Wazhienki Palace, which was magnificent and very large. It was located in a park setting in the style of all European palaces.

Of course, not all parts of the city were as beautiful. There were Christian and Jewish neighborhoods that were quite poor and rundown. In some of them, there was no running water and no indoor plumbing.

In my time, the population of the city was one and a half million people. One-third of them, or approximately 500,000, was Jewish.

Many of the Jews were hard workers, very poor. They lived in Jewish neighborhoods. There were also families of better means, rich ones, as well as many intellectuals. Jews in Poland represented every section of the religious spectrum from Hassidim to people who didn't practice the religion at all.

Whatever their means, the Jews of Warsaw and other parts of Poland were at the epicenter of Jewish life in Eastern Europe.

There was a fine social life. There were many Jewish newspapers, great theatres, libraries, and private schools. In short, when I was a young girl, in spite of the rampant anti-Semitism throughout Poland, I experienced Jewish life as alive and vital and thriving in Warsaw.

All of this was before September 1939.

Let me take this opportunity to tell you a little bit about my background and life situation even before I was born. My family came from a wealthy, cultured background. In Poland there were classes. In my personal surroundings, each and every boy, with the exception of the ones who went to America, had married girls with lots of money. All the boys went to *Yeshiva*, and the girls to private schools as well. This was true for the children of both my mother and father's families. My father's sisters went to school outside the house, but my mother's family had tutors for the girls inside the home. They learned piano and languages.

I know about my grandparents mostly from my parents. I know that my mother's parents, Shlomo Kuperman and his wife, Esther, were born in Warsaw. Both of them were orphans raised by rabbis so they had a religious background. They were married very young and supposedly, my little grandmother, who married my very tall, very large grandfather, was the brains of the family.

She was the one who, instead of my grandfather going into a *shul* and becoming a practicing rabbi, encouraged him to go into business. Their business was scrap metal. They bought discarded metal objects from peddlers and kept them in a yard. They then sold these to big companies. They were very successful at this and made a good deal of money.

After a while, my grandfather went into another business and became one of the first Jewish builders of apartment buildings in Warsaw.

My mother's parents had seven children. Five were girls. The first was Regina, then my mother, Fraida, then Gucha, Sala and Baila. The eldest and youngest in the family were boys. Itzhak or as we called him, Itcha, was the eldest; and the youngest was Samuel.

Because my grandparents were wealthy, they kept us in their home, which was very large and supported our family completely for ten years. Not only did they do this with my mother, they did it for all the sisters in the family. Each of them married very young. The eldest sister, Regina, married a rabbi. Their last name was Kutner.

This rabbi had a *shul* (synagogue) of his own and he was fanatically *frum* (religious).

As a child of six or seven, I visited my uncle's apartment with my mother. When he came in the room, he sat down on a chair with his back to my mother and spoke to us.

He did this because, even though she was his sister-in-law, she fit his definition of a "strange woman," one at whom he should not look.

I knew nothing of this thinking and so ran around in front of him and asked "Why do you talk to my mother and not look at her?"

My mother went "Shish" and I let it go; but his son, about my age, then ran through the room past her and myself without looking at us.

I was very confused. I think I still am.

The rest of the sisters were given enough dowry, apartments, furniture, etc. and went into business. They were all white-collar workers and did very well in business. Gucha's husband was in the jewelry business. Sala and Baila owned fabric stores. The eldest brother had an apartment building and made his living off this. The youngest one was really an artist, a painter. I really don't know exactly what he did, but he lived very well also.

My mother's two brothers traveled a lot before they got married. The youngest one, I remember well.

The eldest brother, Itcha, was married later and wasn't as religious as the rest of the family. He would take money from the business — from the safe — and just disappear. Later, they would get a letter from him that he was in some country — either in Europe or the U.S. He also traveled to South America and Palestine. He was a very handsome man.

I overheard my father say to my mother once that if you would take all of Itcha's children from all over the world, he would have an Army. I guess he was a bit of a playboy.

The youngest son also traveled a lot. He got married when I was about ten years old. That means he must have been in his late 30's. He was a dreamer, an artist and did some painting after he was married. I think he was in business in the stock market as well. They called it the berza.

On the other side, in my father's family, I recall my father's mother only vaguely. I can't remember her name, only that she died in 1940 because of the war. She wasn't a youngster. She was in her 70's and for that time, this was pretty old.

I remember that all her children treated her like a queen. I can still see her lovely apartment on Zlota Street. I also recall she was very jealous of her sons' children and we always heard her talking about her sons. I never had a close relationship with her. I know that she was a lady who read and wrote a few languages, so she must have had a good education as a young girl. She came from Jewish society people.

My mother said that my grandfather, who died before I was born, supposedly was a great man and a very lovable person. Unfortunately, I never knew him. Even worse, there was not even one picture of him, not a painting, nor a photograph. I think he was an ordained rabbi but also had a furniture business.

There were four brothers and three sisters — seven altogether in the Zyskind family. The eldest was my father, Moshe. The next one whose name I don't know went to America and died during the Depression. The third was Feivel, who was called Fabian, and the youngest was Nathan. The sisters were Regina, Cesia (Saysia) and Helen.

After my father was Regina. She was a sweet lady, a great aunt when I needed someone the most after losing all my other close family. She took me in even though I was filthy and hungry.

Next was Feivel. He was a very handsome and dashing guy. My aunt, Mania, his wife, was not nearly as attractive as Feivel. Her mother had been very anxious for Feivel to become her suitor. They were wealthy people in the furniture business with a factory and a store. Her mother, Bobcha, (I called her "grandmother") was a wonderful woman - very attractive, smart, always dressed beautifully, and she spoke a wonderful French as well as Yiddish, Russian and Polish and played the piano. I loved her so much. To me she was the grandma that my own grandma was not. Bobcha was a widow. She was the one who operated the business.

As my Aunt Helen told the story, Bobcha engineered Mania's marriage by inviting Feivel to come to stay at their house in Warsaw. After he came, Bobcha left for a vacation. Feivel and Mania were, at the ages of 22 and 20, left by themselves in this large house. Mania got pregnant and this prompted their marriage. When the first daughter, Baila, was born, she was announced to be premature.

They lived in Warsaw until 1938 and were the smartest of the family. They sold the factory and the business before immigrating to Israel (which was Palestine at the time). They had two daughters, Baila and Hela. When I was reunited with them in Israel in 1950, they were the first people I encountered since the uprising who even knew who I was.

The next child was Nathan, a bookkeeper. His wife, whose name I do not remember, was a member of the wealthy Wolanov family, which sold lottery tickets. She contracted tuberculosis and she was not permitted to nurse their only child, David, and could touch him only when she was wearing a mask. She died before his bar mitzvah. He was raised first by a wet nurse and then by a succession of nannies and housekeepers and sent to a private school.

Nathan eventually started a trucking business, which ran between Warsaw and Bialystok. David became a troublesome child, hated the woman his father subsequently married and joined the Hashomer Hatzair (Zionist Pioneers.) He moved in 1938 to Palestine, became an engineer and was made rosh (leader) of a kibbutz there.

My Uncle Nathan sent his son $10,000, which David gave to the kibbutz. Nathan wanted to emigrate to Palestine and his son said "Here you can't sit around and do nothing, you must learn a trade - this isn't Warsaw where you can collect money without doing anything." That was the reason that Uncle David didn't go to Palestine. During the war, Nathan escaped to Russia and never came back. I have no idea what happened to him.

My father was the only one of his family who was an ordained rabbi. He went to the famous *Shapiro Yeshiva*. The rest of them were secular European people and weren't very religious.

Now that you know about all my father's family, let me add that the only ones who survived were my Uncle Feivel and Aunt Manya, who went to Palestine; and Aunt Helen, who was already in the United States. All the rest of them, including their children, were killed during the Holocaust.

My Aunt Helen was the youngest of my father's sisters. She was a bookkeeper in Warsaw. Because they were afraid she would go out with some boys that they wouldn't approve of, the parents sent her to America to the older brother and asked him to take care of her.

They had one son named Irving. He lives on Long Island now and is my age. I talk to him now and then. He is an engineer; his wife is a teacher. They have three children, two are married and I attended the weddings, of course. The daughter is a violinist, playing in the symphony orchestra. One son is a chemist and the third child, also a son, is an accountant.

CHAPTER 2

My Immediate Family

My father believed that one should read everything that was written, even some ideas that were forbidden for orthodox Jews to read.

My mother, Fraida Kuperman, was very young when she married my father, Moshe Zyskind. I believe she was no more than 16. My father was 17. This was an arranged marriage. Once my grandparents arranged the marriage, they wanted the bride and groom to see each other before the wedding day, so they worked out for the children to each walk with their parents in the park. The plan was that the two families would see each other and this way the children would be able to get a look at their intendeds.

Unfortunately, my father ran away and the plan didn't work. My mother told me that his mother was calling "Moshe, come here." He didn't listen and just ran off. When they got home, my grandma asked her son how he liked the future wife. He said she was "Okay;" but on further questioning, it turned out that he had actually looked at his future mother-in-law, not his future wife. He really had no idea what my mother looked like before the wedding.

So in reality, the first time my father ever really saw my mother was on their wedding day.

They got married in 1905 in Warsaw. My maternal grandparents supported the couple completely for 10 years. I'm not sure exactly what my father did during this time. I assume he studied at least part of the time.

Let me tell you a little bit about my mother and father. This won't be easy for me to say, because this involves the two people whom I loved the most in my life as a child. Besides being a rabbi, my father was a great educator, a man who studied all his life. He spoke, wrote and read Russian, German, Polish, Hebrew and Yiddish fluently and, in addition, he spoke a little French. My father believed that one should read everything that was written, even some ideas that were forbidden for orthodox Jews to read. Specifically, Spinoza, a Jewish philosopher who converted to Christianity, was totally off limits for them to study. But my father believed you should read everything and read his writings.

I remember in 1939 my father began to study Einstein and I said that so few people could understand his writings. My father replied that you can't say you don't understand the writings if you haven't tried to read them. That's the kind of person he was and part of the reason I adored him so much.

My father was five foot eight or nine inches and wore glasses. They were not thick, but he could not see without them, even across the room. He was somewhat heavy set and had a beautiful smile. He loved to tell jokes and had a story for every occasion.

He had a beard and mustache and wore European clothes, except on high holy days, when he dressed in Hassidic ones.

My mother, who looked up to him as though he were a god, was the sweetest person. She was really an angel, a beautiful individual and a wonderful mother, who would do anything and everything for her children. I never remember her raising her voice or doing any harm to anyone. She gave a lot of money to *tzedukah* (charity.)

She was not a person who ever talked loud. Once she found a wallet on the street. I do not know how much was in it. My mother tried to find the owner, but when she could not, she took the money and split it up among beggars. She was truly a great and loving person.

When my mother was young, she had typhoid and it left her with some difficulties. Even though her whole family had a good education, it was difficult for her to study and keep up because of the problems caused by illness.

She adored my father and looked up to him very much. If I asked my mother a question that she wasn't sure of, she would tell me to ask my father. My mother always deferred to my father, feeling that he was more intelligent. She dressed beautifully and kept a lovely house and my father treated her like a china doll. Their marriage was a very good one.

My parents had four children. In 1908, my oldest brother, Itzhak, was born. In 1915, my younger brother Chaim was born. Supposedly, there was one more child before me who died. This child was never spoken of in our home. In fact, I only learned about this child after the war when my cousin told me about it. I was born in 1925 and was the only daughter and last child in the family. I was called Baila (in Polish, Basia, and, in English, Barbara) after my mother's grandmother.

My oldest brother, Itzhak, was a very bright person. It wasn't easy for a Jewish boy to get into the polytechnic institute (similar to the Illinois Institute of Technology), but he got in. He graduated from the institute and became an electrical engineer. He never got married. He moved out of the house a few years before the war. During the war he came back and lived with us. My other brother, Chaim, was a wonderful person. He worked in a machinery parts business that my parents opened for him. He was very happy there.

There was a draft in Poland, and Itzhak, because he was a college graduate, would have entered the army as an officer. Because they didn't want too many Jews as officers, they never selected him for service. Chaim, by the age of 21, was called to army service. My parents were very upset at the prospect of his going off to the army because of the anti-Semitism in Poland. My father went to the head rabbi and they blessed my brother. On the day of his medical exam, my father went to the *shul* and prayed and they burned candles at home hoping this would help keep him out of the army.

Of course, Chaim was strong and healthy and was inducted into the army. He went to the army a few months before *Pesach* in 1937. While he was in the army, he had a dream about a street where a doctor lived. Supposedly, this doctor could help people avoid military service. When he awoke, he looked up the doctor and actually found him on that street. This was a Jewish doctor who understood the plight of Jewish men in the army and how difficult it was for them.

The doctor discovered that, even though Chaim wrote with his right hand, he was really left-handed. At that time, they only took right-handed people into the army. The doctor proposed a simple solution—that he should do everything with his left hand. That way, they would discover that he was left-handed and hopefully, let him go home. And that's exactly what happened.

The family was sitting at our *Pesach* seder and heard a knock on the door. The maid opened the door and there stood Chaim, unrecognizable because his head was shaved. He had civilian clothes and told us now he was released from service. Everyone was so grateful and excited to have him home. This made our holiday even better than before.

Chaim went back to his business and life returned to normal for everyone. One day, I asked Chaim to stop in to a grocery store to buy me some raisins I had seen. When he came home with them, he thanked me. I had no idea why he was thanking me.

A few weeks later, he asked me to come to a coffeehouse. I didn't understand why. I was only 12 years old at the time. At the coffeehouse, he was with a young lady. He told me he met her in the grocery store while he was buying my raisins.

The three of us went to a play and took the young lady home in a carriage. That's when he asked me what I thought of her and told me that he loved her and wanted to marry her. My father didn't want them to marry. Because Poland was a very class-conscious society and she was not in the same class as we were, he was against the marriage.

My brother told my father a few days later that he wanted to bring the girl home to introduce her to the family. My father was against this. My brother pointed out to my father that he had said that this girl was a wonderful saleslady and how much he liked her. My father agreed that she was a good saleslady but added that the tavern likes a drunk, because he brings in money, but certainly doesn't want him as a son-in-law. My brother was terribly hurt. He left the house.

After this, I went to my father and talked to him. I was very nervous to do this because children were not supposed to contradict their parents in those times. But I had a special relationship with him and I knew I had to say this.

I said, "Assume that he doesn't marry this girl and marries someone else. He'll never be happy and he'll always blame you." In addition, I told my father that she was a nice girl.

My father looked at me with tears in his eyes. He said, "My child, G-d gave me some children, but even G-d makes mistakes. He gave me a son who should wear a skirt (meaning he wasn't so smart) and gave me a daughter who should wear pants (meaning she's smart)."

But after this, he relented and accepted the young lady into our family.

Chaim brought the girl home. She had a father and four sisters. They were poor people so we made the wedding. My brother bought an apartment and they were very happily married. They had a baby, a beautiful little girl, at the beginning of 1939.

I had been born in 1925.

My hair was blond and in braids. By the time I was teenager, I had almost reached five feet tall, but I never ever did.

I was a very happy child, who loved music. My mother called me a "chatterbox." If I ever started talking, it was not easy to stop.

My first memories are approximately at the age of three or four years old. I remember a wedding. It was either my mother's cousin's or my oldest cousin's. It was winter and I remember that my parents didn't want to take me to the wedding. However, they prepared my clothes for the wedding just in case they would change their minds. They put me to sleep for a nap and when I awoke I saw the clothes and began crying that I wanted to go. I was a very spoiled little girl and finally, they decided to take me with them. We had a maid and she and my mother helped dress me for the wedding.

To this day, I remember the dress. It was white satin with short sleeves and a blue ribbon around the waist. I had blue ribbons in my long hair to match. It was winter, so I wore a warm coat. My parents were all dressed up as well and this was the first and only time I saw my father wearing a *shtreimel*. Because there was snow on the ground, we went to the wedding in a sleigh.

I remember the music and the bride and the dancing. I remember the *chupah*. It was outside on a terrace. For the dinner, some of the less religious people were sitting in the big ballroom with men and women together. The orthodox women were sitting in the big ballroom as well, but the orthodox men were in a separate room.

The hall was very beautiful with a wonderful orchestra including a violin and piano. In the big ballroom the couples and the children were dancing to the music. In the second room the men were not dancing. The wedding was so beautiful, that to this day, I don't believe I've ever seen such a beautiful wedding.

My childhood was very pleasant. I do not remember my brothers being children. To me, they were always grown-up. Remember that the brother who was closest to me in age was eleven years older than I was.

As a child, my father taught me how to read and write and by the age of five, I was reading and doing some writing. I went to a private pre-school at the age of four. My parents did this because my brothers were so much older and this would give me the opportunity to be around young children.

CHAPTER 3

Polish Anti-Semitism

*Because of what was happening in Germany
and because of the anti-Semitism in Poland,
many Jews wanted to liquidate their businesses
and get out of Poland as soon as possible.
Unfortunately, no country would accept the Jews.
In addition, it was very difficult to get an exit visa
to leave Poland.*

By the age of seven, I began school. I never went to first or second grade but began with third grade. Because my father taught me to read and write, I was able to pass a test and skip first and second grades.

We lived in a predominantly Christian neighborhood; the public school that I went to had only two Jewish children in my class. Schools in Poland were open six days a week, including Saturday. Sunday was the only day off. In Jewish neighborhoods, however, Saturday was the day off and everyone attended school on Sunday. My father wanted me home on Saturday for *Shabbat* and he arranged with the principal of the school for me to take Saturdays off. The principal said this was permissible if I were able to keep up with the class.

About two weeks after I began school, I was introduced to Polish anti-Semitism. The teacher told everyone in the class that they must use their given names and not nicknames that they were called on the street. My nickname was Basia, which was a very Polish name. My given name was Baila — a very Jewish name.

Because I had to use this name, the children realized that I was Jewish and those who were my friends, playing and talking with me one day, began making fun of me with anti-Semitic remarks.

This upset me very much. I came home crying and swearing I wouldn't go to school any more. Because of this, my parents decided to send me to Jewish private school called Paprocka Gymnasium. The school had a number that I remember to this day. We wore it on our coat or dress. The number was 152. The younger children wore a blue number and the older ones in the last two years of high school wore a red one.

This school included elementary, junior high and high school. It was private and attended only by Jewish children, but it wasn't a religious school and we didn't learn religious subjects or Hebrew and Yiddish.

My years there were pretty happy. The school was fine, but, as the time went on, I became aware of more and more anti-Semitism in society at large and in my own neighborhood specifically. There were very few Jews in our area, but there was a *shul* and I heard from time to time at *shul* that a Jew would be roughed up or bothered by anti-Semites.

Many Jews had businesses at this time. There was a section of Warsaw that was populated mostly by Jewish businesses. I remember Swientokrzyska (Shventokshista) Street which had bookstores all owned by orthodox Jews. They had all kinds of books, not just Hebrew. Sometimes they had signs in the window; sometimes there was nothing outside. But, in 1935, a new law was instituted which forced all businesses to write the name of the owner on the front of the business.

This was done specifically so Poles could identify Jewish businesses and boycott them. The same year, I think in the winter, one night, all the windows in the Jewish bookstores were broken. Everyone knew that Polish anti-Semites did this, but nobody was ever found or arrested. Either at the end of 1937 or the beginning of 1938, the mayor of Warsaw made a statement saying that even though beating Jews was illegal, boycotting Jewish businesses was fine with him.

At that same time, another anti-Jewish law set a quota for the amount of meat that could be slaughtered under rabbinic law, thus severely limiting the amount of kosher meat available to the Jewish population. Again, this was a law enacted strictly to make life more difficult for Jews.

Our situation was a little different from some of the other people. As I said, we lived in a predominantly gentile neighborhood. My father always tried to help the people in the neighborhood. These people, while they might want to harm other Jews, considered us "their Jews" and would do nothing to hurt us. Still, they didn't do much to help us either.

By this time, we were hearing about Jews being attacked all over Warsaw. It wasn't safe in some parks or on many streets.

In that same year, at the University of Warsaw, where there was always a quota for Jews, things began to deteriorate as well. The Jewish students were told to sit on the left side of the classroom. The significance of the left side is because Jews were thought to be leftists politically and Communist-leaning. The Jewish students objected to this and many fights broke out. In the end, the Jewish students were forced to sit separately and fighting continued between Jewish and non-Jewish students.

The professors and administrators turned their heads away from this and wanted nothing to do with it. They pretended not to see any of it.

In the same year, 1938, we began to hear news from Germany that Jews who had lived in Germany many years, but didn't have German citizenship, would be sent back to the country where they were born. This meant that many Jews, who had been born in Poland but spent most of their lives in Germany, would have to return to Poland. In fact, these people were physically thrown out of Germany.

Many times this separated families. For example, a husband who was born in Poland and a wife who was born in Germany would be separated.

We also heard very bad news about Hitler's regime. We heard about *Kristalknacht,* the night of broken glass, when Hitler's thugs ran wild destroying Jewish businesses and burning books as well as entire synagogues and preventing anyone from coming to the aid of Jews.

Because of what was happening in Germany and because of the anti-Semitism in Poland, many Jews wanted to liquidate their businesses and get out of Poland as soon as possible. Unfortunately, no country would accept the Jews. In addition, it was very difficult to get an exit visa to leave Poland.

At this time, if a Jew could find a place that would accept him, he could get out of Poland. My Uncle Faval and my father had visas for Palestine. My uncle liquidated his whole furniture business, sold his apartment and left Poland with his family. My father tried to do the same thing, but it took him a lot longer and we weren't able to escape.

CHAPTER 4

The Initial Phase of the War

The wonderful meaning of living was taken from us.

September 1, 1939, is a day I remember vividly. It was a beautiful, sunny Friday; I was walking down the street on the way to buy books for school. As a young girl, I was singing — something I loved to do. I stopped in a bakery and bought a piece of cake to eat.

Suddenly, I heard and saw lots of airplanes flying in the skies over Warsaw. My first thought was that these were Polish airplanes doing training exercises. But these were not Polish airplanes, they were German. I heard noises, not knowing exactly what they were. I was frightened and didn't know what to do; so I ran home.

At that moment the war began. We had been hearing talk about war, but we were not prepared for it when it began.

My father was home, as well as my oldest brother and, of course, my mother. My father thought the war wouldn't take too long, and that it would be over quickly, but that possibly we would have to change our lifestyle somewhat. But he was optimistic that we would survive and that life would soon come back to normal. How wrong he was!

The Germans knew the Jewish neighborhoods and targeted them, bombing Jewish apartment buildings and businesses before any other.

At this time, my brother Chaim—who was married and had a little child—lost his apartment in the bombing. In fact, Chaim, his wife and the child came out of the bombing with one diaper—everything else was destroyed. They came to us to live at this time.

My grandmother's apartment building had been bombed as well and she came to live with us.

Luckily, our apartment had not been bombed. So, we now had eight people living in our house. Poland was occupied by the Germans in about three weeks. Warsaw, itself, was fighting a little longer, but in a month, the Germans came to the city.

Many years ago, I read *The Diary of Anne Frank*. It was long after my own experiences. As was I, Anne Frank was a young teenager during the Nazi occupation. Even though she was writing about what was happening each day, the writing in her diary, I found, something very poetic.

Of course in reading it, I found myself identifying with her. When you are a young girl you want more than anything else for something beautiful to happen to you. You believe you will find a beautiful love. A handsome man will come into your life. You await it.

When does this start? Before you are ten years old, I guess. I remember those years and this hope. I too wrote a diary, which I started when I was eight years old; but ended when the war broke up my life.

The pages no longer exist, but I vividly recall an experience I wrote down on them when I was about 12 years old. I described a beautiful dream that I had had. I was in a place with high mountains. The water, which was blue, was coming down from them in streams and over waterfalls. I was sitting with someone whom I loved very much and who would come into my life, understand me and become my friend and my advisor. I woke up and saw life becoming as beautiful as it was that particular moment.

Anne Frank was waiting for something like this. You see yourself as a young bride in pink. Your life is meaningful because of what is going to happen to you. Then, somebody takes away from you not only these things, but even the dreams. This thing from her life and from mine is something through which I identified and connected with her.

It was for me at this point that the dark came. And when it did, I started to blame my parents, mostly my father. Why had we stayed there? Why didn't he do something to get us out of there?

I remember I asked him once, "Why didn't you do more?" It was 1940 and it was already bad.

He said, "My child, I wish I could have seen what was going to happen, that it was going to be so bad." He didn't see this, however, until after they threw us out of our house. Only then did he fully understand. By then he had one son gone and the other with the baby also gone.

The whole world was upside down. Everything went from a life with color to one that was dark and ugly. The wonderful meaning of living was taken from us.

I did have a taste of it, of the future as it might have been for me. I was 14 years old and went to a movie with Sapka, my best friend. We met two boys there who were very nice. They were a couple of years old than we were. We started to talk. It was in the summer, June 1939, just before the Germans invaded Poland.

One was named Mark and we talked and I enjoyed talking with him very much. We grew fond of one another in the way boys and girls do.

One day, he and I went together to Paderewski Park in Warsaw. It had a small lake and canoes. We rented one and paddled out into the water. We were showering each other with compliments and he kissed me. It was the first time I had ever been kissed and I remember it to this day.

He would come over to our home and I would go down and talk with him. We started to care for each other very much. The war had started and food, very scarce. He brought us, I remember, a half of loaf of bread.

One day, he came over. It was the day after *Yom Kippur*. He was crying. His older sister, her husband and their child had been in *shul* when a bomb destroyed the place. His sister and her husband survived, but the baby was killed. It was the first personal tragedy I had experienced. It was beyond what I could understand.

Mark was really upset. He wanted to go to Russia to fight the Germans like a lot of people were doing. He asked me to go with him. The mayor of the city had urged people to go east and form a new army with which to fight the Germans. I told Mark I would talk to my parents. I did but my father said it was completely out of the question as far as he was concerned.

Mark left and I stayed.

As luck would have it, I encountered him after the war. He was a captain in a Polish unit of the Russian Army. I told him I was married. He asked me to leave my husband. I said I couldn't and we never saw each other again.

When the Germans had marched into Warsaw, I was in the house as was my entire family. We were very frightened about what would come next. We talked and prayed and tried to understand what had happened and what would happen to us in the future.

Many new laws were instituted. One of the first was to close all Jewish schools. No Jewish child was allowed to go to any school. A few months later, Jews were told they had to give up their valuables: gold, silver, antiques, furs. If you refused to give these things up, you could be punished by death. We gave away a little and kept some things because it would be impossible for us to live if we didn't have these things to sell.

With the next law, we had to turn in our radios and telephones, leaving us with no communications. Everything was punishable by death. Most people gave a little away and held back some things to insure their own survival.

With the money that we had left, we bought some food — necessities. There was no bread. My older brother, Itzhak, was standing in line to get bread during the bombing. A piece of shrapnel hit his leg and he was wounded. Some people brought him home.

My other brother, Chaim had his business destroyed, so he was without a business or a place to live. A couple of months after the Nazis came to Warsaw, Chaim, at my father's urging, went to the site of his former business and tried to salvage some of the metal pieces of the machinery he once had. He thought, perhaps he could sell this as scrap metal and get some money for food. While he was doing this, the Nazis found him and beat him so severely that we couldn't even recognize him when he came to our apartment later that evening.

He never spoke of this incident, but he was never the same person again.

At the same time, my older brother, Itzhak who had been hit by a piece of shrapnel, was suffering with an infection in his leg. We found a doctor who told us that we must amputate his leg or he would die. Itzhak would have none of this and said he would rather die than have his leg cut off. A very strange accident occurred a few days later.

It was quite crowded in the house and sometimes people were in each other's way. Itzhak wasn't walking well because he was in pain and I didn't realize that he wanted to sit down. I took the chair away and he fell. He hit his leg and was screaming in pain. At this time the sore opened and all the pus came out. The whole family began to help clean his wound. In the end, this was probably the best thing that could have happened, as the infection was cleaned. Even though the shrapnel in his leg was never removed, he was able to walk again after he recovered.

During this time we were spending money, but no money was coming into the household. After Itzhak was feeling better, he decided that in order to help get some money for the family and being an electrical engineer, he would build a mill to grind grain or corn and possibly this would bring in a little money. He built the mill in a burned out building so as not to alert anyone to what he was doing. This was illegal according to the occupation laws of the Nazis.

One day, before he began to use the mill, some people told us that the Germans knew about his mill and were looking for him. If they caught him he could be arrested and possibly killed. When Itzhak came home, we told him about this and, know what could happen to him, he decided not to go back to the mill.

He stayed at home a few hours, packed a little suitcase, kissed us all goodbye, and left Warsaw to save his life. He planned to go to Russia where he could get away from the German army. After he left a Nazi SS man and a Polish policeman came to find him. After checking the house, they both left, which was a small miracle in itself that they didn't harm any of us.

I never saw my brother again. After the war, I tried for many years to find out his fate, but to this day, I do not know what happened to him. Until a few years go, I never said *kaddish* for Itzhak because I always was dreaming and praying that somehow, somewhere, I would find him alive. But I finally realized that by now, he would be a man in his 90's and so I decided I must now say *kaddish* for him.

The situation went from bad to worse. In January 1940, two SS men came to our apartment. They decided that they liked our place and wanted to live there.

I do not remember if they gave us a few hours or a whole day to leave our place, but we were kicked out and allowed to take only the few things we could carry with us. We were not allowed to take any of the furniture, paintings, rugs or anything from the house.

Luckily, a friend of my father's in a Jewish neighborhood had an empty apartment on Ceglana Street. The people who had lived there left for Russia. We were allowed to move in. It was a pretty nice place. We had three rooms and a kitchen with running water, a toilet and even a bath, which for Warsaw, was a luxury apartment. We didn't have our apartment, but were allowed to use the furniture in the apartment.

All of our family came to live in this apartment. There were seven of us: my father, mother, brother Chaim and his wife and child, my grandmother and me. No money was coming in. Whatever money we had we spent on food. We were selling jewelry, piece by piece. We saw that there was no possible way a baby could survive in Warsaw. There was no milk and my niece's chances were not good.

We discussed this situation and my father and mother decided the best thing to do was send Chaim and his family to the village his wife came from. Possibly in this small town where she had family, they would be able to find food for the baby.

So Chaim and his family left Warsaw. I never saw my sister-in-law or the baby again. I was to see my brother later under terrible circumstances.

Warsaw was no longer the city that I remembered as a child. Under the circumstances, all the things I loved about Warsaw were forbidden for Jews. We couldn't use public transportation and we had to walk in the street if a German was passing by. Normal life was gone. Most of our rights, our possessions and our freedoms were taken from us. We were forced to wear white armbands inscribed with a blue Star of David to identify us as Jews.

Every time they took away something tangible, a bit of our dignity and self-confidence went with it. All of my dreams were taken away. I didn't see a future any more and began to lose my belief in the goodness of human beings. As a young girl with a boundless future I saw the world in many beautiful colors. Now I saw everything in black.

We could not see the beauty of the city any more. All we knew was hunger and our only thoughts were how to get some money or food to survive another day.

In 1940, my grandmother, Esther (my father's mother) died of natural causes. She was in her 70s or 80s. We were able to give her a normal burial.

PART II

The Years of Conflict

CHAPTER 5

The Waraw Ghetto

I know a great deal has been written about the
Warsaw Ghetto, but there are no words to adequately
describe the horror and tragedy that took place
on such an enormous scale.

Around the middle of 1940 the *Judenrat* was formed. This was a committee of prominent Jewish men who were attempting to deal with the political, social and economic conditions for Jews, which were deteriorating every day. The head of the *Judenrat* whose name was Chernikov. He was one of the most dedicated, caring people I knew. He truly had a Jewish soul and a Jewish heart. He tried to help the people, even though he was used by the Nazis to carry out many of their outrageous demands on the Jews. Sadly, later he would come to a tragic end.

In the beginning of 1941, the Nazis decided that all the Jews had to live in a ghetto. Actually, the Jews were physically building the walls of the ghetto themselves. Jews who were not living in the ghetto had to move into it and were required to exchange apartments with those Poles who lived in the confined area. No attention was paid to the size or equity of the exchange. Someone with a very large apartment could easily be required to exchange it for a one-room apartment without any compensation.

The ghetto was the poorest Jewish neighborhood in the city. The area originally held 100,000 people. At its height, the Warsaw Ghetto would contain 500,000, so you can imagine how horrible conditions became.

The ghetto. I know a great deal has been written about the Warsaw Ghetto, but there are no words to adequately describe the horror and tragedy that took place on such an enormous scale. This was a place unfit for human habitation. How can I express my own feelings? I felt that I was going to a prison from which I would never escape. It was a place that reminded me of what I imagine the Dark Ages were like. I didn't think in these modern times that people were capable of treating other people in such an inhuman manner. I never will forget the smell, the cries and the dead people on the street. To get where you were going, you had to walk around bodies lying on the sidewalk.

The children—they looked like blown up balloons with yellow faces—so sick they were not even able to cry any more.

Now when I see pictures of starving children in Africa, it reminds me of the babies in the Warsaw Ghetto. I thought, even if I survive all of this, how could I ever be myself again? What kind of human being would I be after seeing so much tragedy? How could I ever be the same person I was before?

At this time, the Nazis gave food stamps to the whole population — for Poles and Jews. The difference was that on our stamps there was a big "J." We also got about 25 percent of the amount the Poles were getting. What we were allowed to get, we had to pay for as well. We had to buy food on the black market because the amount we were allotted was not enough on which to survive. The black market was very expensive.

The black market food was brought to the ghetto through basements in bombed-out buildings. The smugglers were able to make a lot of money but this was dangerous for them even though they were not Jewish. There were some Jewish smugglers as well. In fact, all the smugglers risked their lives.

I should mention also the little children who were able to smuggle food into the ghetto from the Aryan side. They did this in an ingenious way. The wall around the ghetto was all brick. The children went with a companion to a corner of the wall that was not heavily guarded. They loosened a few bricks, removed their armbands and crept quietly over to the Aryan side while the companion replaced the bricks. These children were usually around eight or nine years old. They were old enough to understand what they had to do, but small enough to sneak through. Then they walked the streets begging or looking for food. If they were successful, they returned to the ghetto undetected. In this way, they were able to keep their families alive. Of course, many of the children were caught and murdered by the guards. But many families were in such dire straits that they felt there was no other choice.

Often people did not have enough money to purchase something to eat. This was when we began to see people fighting each other for food. The result was that many people starved to death.

Jews were required to wear a white armband with a blue Star of David in the middle. If you were caught without this, you would be killed. I would like to explain a little bit about why we wore this armband and the circumstances of the time. In Poland, going back many generations, everyone had to register new births with the authorities. It was required to give your religion on this form. Therefore, the authorities knew everyone's religion.

When the Nazis took over, of course, it was easy for them to recognize the more religious Jews such as Hasidim, because of their unique clothing, but secular Jews were much more difficult to recognize. In this regard, many Poles helped the Germans identify who, indeed were Jews. The Poles knew it was especially good for them to point out a Jew without an armband. This would give the Pole a reward from the Nazis such as extra food. Some of the Poles would do this without any reward because of their anti-Semitism.

In addition, when we went to pick up our food stamps, we were required to wear the armband by law. When you announced your name, it was immediately evident that you were a Jew and leaving the armband at home was punishable by death.

Of course, there were some Polish people who wouldn't point out Jews and some who even helped the Jews. These people risked their lives and were very unique.

Even though the life in the ghetto at this time—1940 and 1941—was harsh and very difficult, there still was some cultural and religious life. Some actors from the Jewish Theatre cleaned up a barn and put on great performances, which I remember to this day. This was actually the first time I'd ever seen a Jewish play and I was really impressed.

My mother was a great housekeeper and cook and was able to make a wonderful meal from almost nothing. But, slowly our resources were being depleted. We were selling jewelry, one piece at a time. Our situation was getting worse every day. No money was coming in and we were running short of valuables to sell for food.

At this time, I was about 15 and I decided I needed to do something to help the family. My father and mother had never done any manual labor in their lives.

I want to say that because I skipped first and second grades, and because I attended a private school, I had more education than the average 15-year-old. Since no schools for Jewish children were allowed to remain open, I decided to begin tutoring young children for which I was paid a little bit of money.

My tutoring continued for several months. Because all the schools were closed, people were desperate and struggled hard to come up with the small fee I charged. It was hard work and I did it for 10 to 12 hours a day. I was very tired, but at least I was making enough money to buy necessities so the family could survive. My biggest reward was not money, but to see bread on the table and know that I was able to help my family survive.

I knew that my father was capable of teaching Hebrew subjects and language to the children, but he could never ask for work. I came to him and asked him to take the children I was tutoring and teach them Hebrew. I said they would pay for this and he would be doing a *mitzvah* (good deed) because of that. I, on the other hand, told the parents of the children that they would have to pay me for the Hebrew tutoring. I collected all the money and for a little while that helped us keep from being hungry.

I will never forget *Rosh Hashana* and *Yom Kippur*, 1940. All services and meetings of any kind, secular or religious, were strictly prohibited. Any infraction was punishable by death.

We were living on Ceglana Street and my father secretly brought one Torah from the synagogue and invited his friends, orthodox Jews, to come pray with us. My father conducted the services and blew the *shofar (ram's horn.)* That was the first time I ever heard him do this and to this day I vividly remember his beautiful voice. Each year when I hear the cantor on the high holidays, it reminds me of my father and the wonderful service he conducted in spite of the many obstacles in his path.

During *Yom Kippur*, while my father was conducting his service, I took a walk outside. There, on the street, I came upon a horrible scene—SS men walking with a group of about 20 orthodox Jews. The man in the lead was wearing a *tallis* (prayer shawl) and carrying the Torah. One of the Nazis shot and killed the man carrying the Torah before my eyes. The others were marched off. After the men and the Nazis left I saw the Torah, our holy book, just lying there in the street. Watching this scene, I became hysterical. I was afraid to be there and ran home. When my father saw how upset I was, he stopped the service. I told the worshippers what I'd just witnessed and there wasn't a dry eye in the room

Everyone said a special prayer for those people and for the man who was killed. Then my father resumed the service. He said that G-d was expecting this of us, and he continued to pray. I asked my father, "Is this the same G-d you're praying to that let this horror happen?" He had no answer — he just kissed me and said, "I still hope we'll survive, my child." That was the *Yom Kippur* I'll never forget.

My father, who loved his books so much, had a special edition of Maimonides' works. He had all the volumes except one. He was looking for this for many years before the war. One day when we were still on Ceglana Street, my father went to buy some food. When he came back, he was all smiles. He didn't return with food, but with that missing volume of Maimonides' works. He had traded the bread for this book. That's how important books were to him.

I told him, "Dad, we need the bread."

"We won't starve without the bread one day," he told me, "but that book, that book, it's a treasure."

There was a newspaper printed in the ghetto. Even though this was illegal, it afforded us the opportunity to get some news of what was going on inside the ghetto.

It pains me to tell this, but there were Jews who policed the ghetto. People would pay great sums of money to get their sons positions as policemen because they thought their lives would be easier. Before he left, my brother Chaim was asked by the federation and the Germans to become a policeman. He hid so as not to be found because he didn't want this position. As I said, he left Warsaw shortly thereafter.

At the beginning, the job of the policeman was to control traffic and make sure that everyone obeyed the laws. Later, the policemen did some very ugly things.

After a while, the situation worsened and people didn't care about tutoring. They were interested merely in surviving. This was, of course, the end of my tutoring job and I temporarily lost the ability to help my parents.

One day I was walking in the ghetto with my friend, Sapka. We were stopped by two Nazis. They took us to an office and told us to clean the office. I asked for some rags to use for cleaning and he told me to take off my underwear to use for rags. I did this and washed the floor with my underwear. I didn't wash the floor to his satisfaction so he beat me with a whip. I lost consciousness. I have no idea who brought me out of that office but when I regained consciousness I was at home with my mother and father standing over me. He beat me so badly that, to this day, I still have scars from that beating. That was my first experience with the Nazis. The important thing is that I survived.

The Jewish smugglers used our balcony to communicate with the Poles. I asked my father why they didn't pay us for using our balcony. If the Nazis found out about this, we would be the ones to suffer. My father said that these people were risking their lives to bring a little food to the Jews and he couldn't ask them for money.

Our family was becoming increasingly desperate so I asked the smugglers to help me make a little money. They told me that if I wanted to sit in the basement where the food was being smuggled in and out, I would be able to sell some food to the smugglers themselves and would be able to charge more than it would cost me to buy this food. In this way, I could make a little money. Of course, this was very risky for me. If the Nazis found me I would be killed. But I felt I had to take this risk to bring some money into the house. I did not tell my parents what I was doing. I told them I was taking care of an old lady and staying in her house some nights and that she was giving me money for this. This all took place in 1941.

The Nazis would come in without warning or reason, and take some people out of the ghetto and kill them. These were random killings. We thought the situation in the ghetto had become unbearable. What we didn't know was that things would get much worse.

The ghetto was shrinking because people were dying of starvation and sickness. There were very few doctors and only one hospital, which was operated by German doctors. Whoever went in there never came out alive. Needless to say, no matter how sick people were, they wouldn't go there.

The food that was smuggled in was so expensive that almost nobody could afford it. There was no coal, no medicine and no soap. Because of this there was a terrible epidemic of typhoid. By the end of 1941, I was ill with it. My parents didn't call a doctor because they knew if they called one I would be taken to the hospital and that would be the end of me.

I was very ill for a very long time—about three months. I was delirious. I remember that I was hemorrhaging from my nose and my ears. My parents were standing near me and my mother was crying and saying, "My baby's dying." I prayed to G-d to help me. I said, "I'm so young, please G-d, let me live. I promise that the first five *zlotys* I get, I will give to charity." It was very bad.

My father put my feet up and my head down and I finally stopped hemorrhaging. But I lost consciousness again. When I did wake up, I saw that the apartment was almost empty. There was also no furniture and all the clothing except for one set of clothes was gone.

CHAPTER 6

The Worst Moment of My Life

I yelled at G-d, "Why are you doing this to us? WHY? WHY? WHY?"

For me, one moment of my life was the worst; far, far worse than any other. It was more horrible and terrifying than when I was hungry, being beaten or even threatened with immediate death. For more 60 years, I blocked it out.

Only after, for a second time, watching the movie, "The Pianist," did it ever come back to me. What had happened more than came back—it broke like a dam and I cried all night long. Strange as it might seem, it was about when I stopped being able to cry.

People, over the years, had asked me what was the worst time ever for me and I readily said that it was when my father died. It was, but the most frightened that I ever was, was a day before that.

While I was sick with typhoid, my family had been forced to leave their apartment. I saw a wagon piled with our few belongings including furniture and books. Someone, I don't remember who, put me on top of all this. They said, "It doesn't make any difference, she won't survive anyway."

I don't remember who pulled the wagon. I was in and out of consciousness at this time. We ended up in one ugly little room. It was an awful ugly, dirty hellhole. The building had many apartments. We had only one room in one of them.

This place was on Pawia Street. There was one bed, one table with three chairs, a stove and some dishes and a small cabinet. That was all we had. I didn't know what I could do for my family. Because of the hemorrhaging, I almost completely lost the vision in one eye.

I think I was getting over the typhoid, but I was so weak I could barely see or walk. My mother, who was such a beautiful lady, was not the same any more. My father as well. I don't remember how or from where, but we got a small amount of bread. We all slept in one bed. We were not clean because we had no way to clean ourselves.

After we first moved in, I started hearing scratching noises. It was a rat, my father told me. It scared me something terrible. I thought it was going to bite me, kill me. I would die not from hunger, disease or the Nazis; but the bite of that rat. Every night when I went to bed, I would pull the blanket up and cover my face so it wouldn't get me there. In the nighttime, I would hear it and wake up. I was certain it was going to get me.

The people in the next room got a cat and I heard it in the middle of the night kill the rat. It frightened me out of my mind. In the back of my head, since then, I think I have associated cats and rats with that incident.

I was a bit better, but by now my father had become ill. He was getting sicker and sicker.

One night he called me to his bed and began talking to me — giving me advice and telling me things that made me begin to feel that he was dying. He told me where to find some papers and who to go live with and I cried and asked him why he was telling me these things. He said that we don't know what will happen and I want you to know these things.

He talked to me all night. He gave me advice on marriage. He told me never to seek money. To illustrate this he said, "If a horse has a bag of money, everyone will bow down to him, but when the money's gone, he's still nothing but a horse." He told me to be sure I married someone nice that was the most important thing. He said to try to recognize that if you marry a bad person, it will come out in an argument or somehow when the person is angry. You won't be able to handle this, so you should beware and not get into this situation. He said, "An average apple from a good tree is better than a fabulous apple from a bad."

It was cold and we had nothing for fuel. "Take my books and burn them," he told me. "Instead of them burning them, you do it." I did, but only some of them.

"Everyone can take from you all of your possessions," he said. "They have to kill you to take away your knowledge."

For a long time, I could recall only a few things of what he had said. Now, I recall more. He said, for example, "My child, the sun never shines just before it gets the darkest. I hope the worst is over for you, that things will get better."

Then, he told me the hardest thing of all. Before the Nazi invasion, he said, he had had papers that would have allowed him to emigrate to Brooklyn as a rabbi. My mother's parent, however, forbade her to go and she listened to them. He said would not go without his family.

"I forgive her for myself," my father told me, "but not for you. As I see you now, I very much know we should have gone. For that, I cannot forgive her."

I understood why he told me all these things. I knew he would die. Something snapped. It was my will to go on.

I became hysterical. I screamed loud and I kept it up. I yelled at G-d, "Why are you doing this to us? WHY? WHY? WHY?"

I must have fallen asleep sitting on a chair next to his bed. When I woke up, I wanted to give him some water to drink. He was in a coma, his eyes were closed. I didn't know what to do. My mother wasn't herself and seemed incapable of acting. So I ran out into the street, found a doctor's residence and begged him to come home with me and help my father. On the way home with the doctor, somehow, I ripped the sleeve of my coat. I took this as a very bad omen. In our tradition, when a loved one dies, the family members tear a piece of clothing to signify that their heart is broken. This upset me very much and I hoped that I wasn't too late.

When the doctor looked at my father he knew even without checking him that it was no longer possible to save him. I don't know how the doctor could have because he had no medicine available to him. The doctor said, "My child, he's dying. Why don't you let him die in peace?" Then he left.

I ran to my father's bed and began crying and screaming, "Don't die, don't leave me here, what should I do?" My father stretched his arms out and hugged me with tears coming from his eyes. He didn't say anything and a few moments later he died. He was 49 years old.

Mama lost her mind. She wasn't the same after that.

"I do not want to live," she said.

Up to this point, I had seen catastrophes happening around me; but, somehow, I felt insulated. At the moment of my father's death, it became personal. I completely broke down. I no longer believed I would be able to survive and didn't know if I wanted to. To me, my life was over. I didn't care about anyone including myself. What had happened changed my entire life.

I ran to my uncle, Rabbi Kutner, and asked him what to do. He told me not to worry that he would send someone. We had a plot in the cemetery, but we were unable to go to there because it was outside the ghetto walls. I didn't have any money and I didn't know what to do. Because so many people were dying every day, there was a wagon that went around. My uncle sent two men. They took my beloved father on a stretcher out to a cart that had other bodies on it. He didn't even get a decent Jewish burial. To this day, I have no idea where he is buried.

After my terrible illness, I was so weak and miserable. I was left with my mother in this ugly, miserable little room. One suit of my father's was left. My mother wanted to sell it because there wasn't even a penny for a piece of bread. She did and got a few *zlotys* and these were stolen from her on the way home. She came without the suit or the money. This seemed to take all the spirit out of her. She seemed to have death on her face.

My brother, Chaim, came to us two days later. He himself smuggled into the ghetto because he had a dream. When he entered, I sensed he was in a new place. I saw it in his face.

"Where's Dad?" he asked.

I couldn't tell him.

"Dad went to pray," I said.

"No," he said. "He called me to say *kaddish*. Dad is dead."

"No," I persisted.

"You're lying," he said. "Dad called me to say *kaddish*."

I do not remember asking him about his wife and child. I felt no emotions. It was as though he and my mother were strangers.

I don't recall very much about what happened next. I only remember two horrible incidents for which I will never forgive myself. I don't know why I acted the way I did. I don't know what made me do this. I hurt the people I love the most and it haunts me to this day.

Sometime after my father died, I ran away from the room we lived in. I don't remember when or why this happened. I do recall that I came to a grocery store in the ghetto and there was a woman who owned the store. She had a child who lived upstairs and she told me she would give me a little to eat if I would sleep in the store and bring food to the daughter.

One day while I was in the store, my mother came in. She looked so close to death, I knew she didn't have long to live. She asked me, with tears in her eyes, to take her to my aunt's house. I refused. I don't know why I did.

Later, I was told that my mother had died at my aunt's house. She was 48. My brother died in the room we had. He was only 26 years old. I never went back to these places to try to see either of them.

I don't remember talking to my brother or asking him about the fate of his wife or child. He came to the store and asked me to give him the food I was holding for the child. He said, "I'm dying, please give it to me." I just ran away.

I have spoken to doctors and rabbis about these incidents and they always tell me that, realistically, even if I walked with my mother, I couldn't have saved her from death. I know my brother would have died even if I had given him that piece of bread. They tell me that I am not to blame for their deaths, that I was little more than a child and in complete fear myself. I understand this intellectually, but I cannot forgive myself, no matter how much I try to rationalize it.

So really, what happened to me? G-d, I will never understand why I did it — why I acted the way I did toward the people I loved the most in this world. I must believe that my grief and fright caused me to act in a way I would never believe I could. I must believe that because I was on emotional overload, everything just shut down and I was unable to feel anything at all.

To this day, I pray G-d for forgiveness. How could I have ignored them in their time of need? I never go to bed without saying a prayer and also asking my mother and brother for forgiveness. I will never understand how it happened.

It wasn't enough that the Nazis took my family, that I was starving and filthy, but they took away all my feelings and changed me into a half-animal. For making me act in this way, I will never forgive the Nazis.

CHAPTER 7

A Time of Unreality

Most of my friends were gone.
I never found out what happened to them.

I think at this time I went into shock. I know there is a period that I simply don't remember. Even more upsetting is that I am unsure about how long this period of time lasted. My best calculations say it was four or five months. I have absolutely no memory of anything that happened during this time.

The next thing I can recall was walking along the street in the ghetto feeling extremely hungry and knowing I was dirty. I don't remember where I was before, where I slept, or when the last time I really washed myself was. Everything was a complete blank. I know it was the winter of 1941-42 at this time, but I don't know what day or month it was. I was walking and thinking how I could get a piece of bread to eat. All I had left was my winter coat, which I was wearing. In it, there was a lining and I decided this was the only thing of value I had left to sell. I sold my lining to a smuggler and received a piece of bread.

I was holding the bread in my hand. Several minutes later, a *"khopper,"* one of the young boys who stole food from people walking down the street, grabbed my bread and ran away with it. These boys were so hungry themselves that, when one grabbed a piece of bread from someone, he would immediately shove it in his mouth and begin eating it. People saw the bread being stolen from me and tried to run and catch the boy. They tried to take away from him what was still the piece of bread. I stopped the people. I walked away in tears without the lining and without the bread. At this time I was 16 years old.

As I was walking along and crying, an older lady stopped me and asked me if I were Basha Zyskind and I said, "Yes." She told me that she knew my parents and I told her that I lost them and all my family and that I was by myself and didn't know where I could go or what to do. She mentioned to me that my Aunt Baila and her husband were still in the ghetto and I should go to them.

I went to Aunt Baila's and told her what happened to the family. She didn't know anything about this. We were both crying and feeling very sad. She shared her bread with me even though she didn't have much herself and told me to stay with her. I knew that she didn't have food to give me. Aunt Baila told me that she knew of a soup kitchen close to her apartment. She encouraged me to go there and try to get something to eat.

A Jewish organization ran the soup kitchen. They had been involved with other activities prior to this, but at this time, the most important thing was to save the children from starvation. I looked much younger than my 16 years and I thought I might be able to get some food there. When I went down there, they let me in and gave me some soup and a piece of bread. They told me that I could come every day for something to eat. I felt terrible, having to take food from the soup kitchen, but there was no other way to survive.

I stayed with Aunt Baila a few months and during this time she asked me to take some soup to my Aunt Sara who lived about 10 blocks away. I carried the soup to her place but she wasn't in her apartment. Some other people were now occupying the place and I was told that my Uncle Hershel, her husband, had died and that she was now staying in the basement. This was a dirty, filthy basement filled with rats and vermin, not an apartment. As I walked closer to it I could see how dark and scary the place was. I went in and saw my aunt lying on a cot. Her appearance frightened me. She had been a beautiful woman and now she was dirty and wild looking. She recognized me and tried to hug me and thank me for the soup. I was so frightened that I just ran away and left her there. Outside I cried hysterically, just thinking "Is this really true, is this really what happened to all my loved ones?" Where was G-d? What had happened?

When I got back to my Aunt Baila, I told her about her sister. I couldn't stay with her much longer because her place was very small and I felt I was imposing on her too much. In this one small room there were four people — my aunt, her husband and two daughters. So I went back to Ceglana Street hoping that I would see one of my friends.

When I got there, most of the apartments had many more people in them than before the war. These were beautiful apartments at one time. I knocked on some doors and there were strange people in the apartments. Most of my friends were gone. I would never discover what happened to them.

Finally, I approached an apartment that had been occupied by the family of a friend of mine. My friend was not there, he had left Warsaw, but I found his older brother there. He asked me to come in and gave me some food. He was a policeman and had quite a bit more food than many other people. I sat and ate and talked with him for a while. I noticed that it was late and had gotten dark. I was fearful of walking alone at night in the ghetto and asked him if I could spend the night there. I had nowhere else to go.

This apartment had two rooms and I noticed that each room had a bed in it. I asked if I could sleep in the kitchen and he agreed to let me stay there. I went to sleep and in the middle of the night I woke up and became aware of my friend's brother touching me and trying to get into bed with me. I started to cry and said, "Please don't touch me." I was so frightened, I told him I was menstruating and that I was a virgin and that I was dirty. I tried every excuse I could think of and cried harder and harder. Finally, he left me alone.

I couldn't sleep any more and when the sun rose and I could see some light, I left. On the way out, in the back yard, I met Kuba, a friend of mine from the Ceglana Street group. I told him everything that had happened to me. He was very sympathetic and told me that his parents, who had a two-room apartment and running water, were out until the end of the day. He told me he would stay downstairs and watch so that nobody would disturb me and allowed me to go to his place and wash up. I did and felt a bit cleaner than before.

Kuba told me about an elderly woman next door who had some food and needed a companion to stay with her. I went to her apartment. She took me in as a companion because she was afraid to be alone. I thought I would stay with her and keep her company. Actually, she wanted a maid. She forced me to clean the windows and wash the floors and sleep in the cold kitchen. I had never done this sort of work before and I probably wasn't too good at it. After a couple of weeks, she forced me to leave.

As I was leaving, about a block away, I thought I saw a familiar face in one of the apartments. When I got closer, I realized that I didn't know any of these people. As I walked around the building, I noticed that there was an empty apartment. I went inside and there was nothing in the apartment except a trunk and a can filled with melted butter. I took the can of butter with me and left. I went to a small place where they were serving food. I asked them if I could trade some butter for soup. I gave them four tablespoons of butter and they gave me a bowl of soup. Another four tablespoons got me a piece of bread. I asked if I could sleep in this place and they allowed me to sleep on a cot in the corner. I slept with my can of butter attached to my arm so nobody would take it. I spent about a week in this place.

CHAPTER 8

A Reflection on Degradation

Even with all the deprivation the Germans had caused and the cruel manner in which they treated us, nobody could believe that they actually intended to kill everyone — men, women and children.

After the war, I returned to Warsaw to see if I could find any record that might help me find where my parents' bodies were buried, and was shown a common grave where thousands of bodies had been dumped. "There are no names," said the man who took me there.

A few of the bodies were encased in wooden boxes, but most were just piled on the handcarts, which had to cross No Man's Land to get to the cemetery. On the way, the carts were checked by police, because people also used them to smuggle things in and out of the ghetto. Such checking was often cursory, however, because the police feared catching typhoid or other infectious diseases from the rotting corpses. I have a friend, who is alive in Skokie today, who as a child was smuggled out in such a coffin.

Were they really human? I still have marks on my face, my neck, my arm, and my hand where they put cigarettes out on me or beat me. There was so much sadism. You see it in the movie. They made us dance, or kiss their feet, or serve as the butt of their jokes. Why did we obey their rules? I really don't know. Was it to survive? Is it because the Jews had become compliant as a result of the pogroms and other catastrophes that had beset us? Why did we wear the Star of David armbands? Why did we not take them off? It was degrading. They had taken away our freedom and dignity. Still, we did things to make them feel a little better in hopes that they would treat us a little better. And, at some level, we began to accept their view that we were lower than they.

And then there were the Jewish policemen, many of whom came from good families. They lived better than we did. They had little cafes in basement. In exchange for these privileges, they had to bring in individuals to be taken to the death camps. Sometimes they would even bring in members of their own families in order to show their loyalty. I knew a little boy named Sigfried, whose father was a German Jew working for the Nazis. He lived like a king, but in the end he and the Jewish policemen all ended up in the same death camps to which they had sent others.

I found out at this time that the Nazis asked Mr. Chernikov, the president of *Judenrat* to work with them and give them a list of people to be deported to "work camps." Mr. Chernikov must have known or at least suspected that the Nazis really wanted to exterminate these people. He rejected them and committed suicide. I am not certain, but I think the rest of the family, a wife and two children, did so as well.

Another man, named Heller replaced Chernikov. Heller was from Lodz. This man worked with the Nazis and delivered people to them.

At this time I was still there I described trading butter for food. I heard that the Nazis wanted to resettle people from the Warsaw Ghetto in a small town in the Polish countryside. The Nazis said they would keep families together and they encouraged everyone to come to *Umschlagplatz* as a central meeting place. They said the trains would be waiting and every family would receive a loaf of bread and some jam.

As we know now, this was a ruse. However, people believed them. Even with all the deprivation the Germans had caused and the cruel manner in which the treated us, nobody could believe that they actually intended to kill everyone — men, women and children. How could we NOT believe that we were being resettled? Life in the ghetto was so terrible—this was our only hope. Nobody would allow him or herself to believe that in the 20th century, this would come from a country like Germany, the most highly educated in all of Europe, a country that gave the world so many great writers, composers, and philosophers. Who could believe that these same people were capable of mass genocide? How could we believe that those intellectuals, those chemists and engineers were capable of producing a complete industry dedicated to killing people?

Jews by the thousands, believing the Nazis and hoping against hope that they were telling the truth, and knowing that they couldn't hold out much longer against hunger and disease in the ghetto, went to the *Umschlagplatz*.

I heard the news and went back to my Aunt Baila's house. We all talked about the offer and they decided to take it and asked me to come along as part of their family. For some reason, I didn't want to go. I have no idea why I said, "No." The following day we said goodbye to each other and I never saw any of them again.

I remember one guy, his name was Rubinstein; he escaped from *Treblinka* somehow and returned to the ghetto. He ran through the streets screaming, "They're gassing us, they're burning us." In the beginning, nobody believed him.

However, after some weeks, people in the ghetto began to be suspicious about what was happening to them who had left for resettlement. Some people from the underground, (which consisted of Jews and non-Jews), followed a train and found that it's destination was 80 miles from Warsaw at a death camp called *Treblinka*. This camp had been created specifically and solely for the purpose of killing people. They were taken in cattle cars in the morning. When they were unloaded, all their belongings were taken from them. The people were sent to be gassed and from there, their remains were moved to the crematorium and burned. The Nazis did this with such precision and clockwork that the trains were able to return empty to Warsaw that same evening.

So Rubenstein had not been crazy. He was trying to warn us. I was completely horrified, as was everyone in the ghetto, when we discovered the truth. Because people found out, they, of course, stopped going to the trains of their own free will.

Such was the Nazi thinking to exterminate every Jewish man, woman and child; so that even though the war was continuing and the Nazis needed men and equipment transported to all the fronts, their top priority was to send trains of Jews to their deaths in the camps

Later, I would walk to the *Umshlagplatz*, where they were loading Jews on cattle cars. A Jewish policeman there, who knew me, grabbed hold of me and asked what I was doing.

"I don't care anymore," I said. "I want to die."

He pulled me into an entranceway and yelled at me to stay there. Leaving me with another policeman, he said, "Watch her. She's crazy."

I started screaming and the man began hitting me.

When the policeman came back, he saw this and demanded to know why I was crying.

The other man said, "You said she was crazy, so I was trying to stop her from screaming."

"No, no," the policeman said. "She's not crazy. She's a friend."

As time went by and the situation got much worse. Handcarts were pushed along the streets to pick up the dead, and they were taken for burial in a mass grave outside the ghetto walls. Until they were picked up, you had to walk around the bodies.

CHAPTER 9

Aktions and Selections

A woman answered, but she would not let me in.
I can imagine now why she would have been hesitant
to unlock the door. I was filthy, and I'm sure she was
afraid I would bring some disease in with me.

Since people now understood what their fate would be, no one was going to the *Umschlagplatz* on their own their own anymore.

Because of this, the Germans devised another way of getting people to come out of the ghetto. They began what were called *aktions*. The Germans would surround a square block with SS troops, and sometimes also with soldiers from areas such as the Ukraine or Lithuania. Then they would take everyone living in the apartments in this square block out of their homes, yelling at them and beating them. No one was exempt; young children, the old, and the sick were all taken. These people were then loaded onto trucks and taken to the *Umschlagplatz*, where cattle cars were waiting to take them to *Treblinka,* a place from which they did not return alive. The *aktions* began in mid-1942 and continued through the uprising in April 1943.

I remember walking on the street and again being hungry and not knowing where I would sleep at night. As before, an older woman stopped me.

She recognized me, and asked about my family. I told here that I had no one, that everyone was gone. She told me there was a lady in one of the nearby buildings who ran a grocery store. In the ghetto, store owners received only enough food to sell on the food stamp rations that were given to people. It was not like a grocery store that we would think of today where you could go and buy anything you wanted, or where the owners would be making good sums of money. Even so, the people who sold groceries were better off because they always had food.

I went to a third-floor apartment and rang the bell. A woman answered, but she would not let me in. I can imagine now why she would have been hesitant to unlock the door. I was filthy, and I'm sure she was afraid I would bring some disease in with me. But can you imagine how this would make a fifteen-year-old girl would feel, someone who had always been clean? At the time, I had long hair, which was always itchy, but I never thought about it. Looking back, I am certain that I had things crawling on me while I stood at that door.

As I was standing there, I suddenly heard shouting, whistles, crying, and screaming all around me, and realized that an *aktion* was taking place on that very block. Immensely frightened, knowing instinctively that I needed to get away from there immediately, I turned and streaked down the stairs. At ground level, I spied some little basement windows, one of which was open, but at the same time one of the German soldiers saw me. Jumping through the window, I found myself in a small room filled with feathers, which immediately covered me when I landed in them. The German began firing into the room, but I lay still, and he finally gave up and walked away. Luckily, I was not hit.

As I lay there under the feathers, I heard shooting and horrible screaming and crying, and I knew that some of the people were dead already. Thinking that the Germans might still be there, I lay there for about two or three hours till it became absolutely quiet. When I did finally venture out, now not only filthy dirty but with feathers stuck to me, I discovered three dead bodies, and was enveloped by an eerie silence. I saw no living person; everyone had been taken away.

As I stood there trying to comprehend what had happened, I saw a young girl emerge from another entrance to the same building. Obviously, she also had been hiding, and we were the only two survivors of this *aktion*. Although I didn't know her, we hugged each other and cried for some time. Upon my telling her why I was in this area, she suggested that we go up and check out the third-floor apartment where I had been sent to. There we found furniture, food, and people's personal effects; everything except the people who had been taken away.

Because we were hungry, food was the first thing on our minds, and we ate quite a bit. In fact, it was difficult to stop eating. There was bread and jam and other things, and we both just ate until we couldn't eat anymore. The other girl was dirty too, though not as filthy as I, and after eating we realized that we wanted to clean up a bit. Finding soap and cold running water, we cleaned ourselves as best we could. My clothes were so disreputable I discarded them, and went into the wardrobe looking for something to wear. We picked through all the woman's clothes, including her underwear, taking anything we could wear. This woman had been much taller than either of us, so I took scissors and cut her dresses down to size. I even took some shoes that were quite big on me, and stuffed them with paper to make them fit better. What we didn't wear, we divided between us, filling two pillowcases each, and then left the building and began walking.

The other girl told me that the Germans had opened several new factories in the ghetto. The one in the small ghetto, called Tebens, made uniforms, and the one in the large ghetto made brooms. These were huge factories, employing more than 20,000 Jews, who received no wages but only food. Between the German bosses and the workers were Jewish supervisors, called *meinsters*.

There was also a factory named The Shultz Factory, which I believe also made uniforms. And then there was a group operating in the ghetto called *Vertifasung*, which, under German supervision cleaned and packed valuables and clothing remaining in apartments where *aktions* had taken place, and prepared them for shipment to Germany.

As I was walking across the bridge connecting the two sections of the ghetto, I was approached by a young boy who offered to carry my two pillowcases, saying that they appeared to be quite heavy. He was very polite, and I was very tired, so I gladly handed him the pillowcases. The next thing I knew, he was gone, along with all the clothes I had. When I looked around, I couldn't find the other girl, so I decided to proceed to Shwientojerska 32, the location of the broom factory.

The broom factory was in an enormous building, which took up an entire square block. Before the war the building had been a shopping arcade, with the central courtyard filled with furriers and clothing merchants. It turned out that the broom factory was just being organized, and the courtyard was filled with people. As I walked through the crowd, I began talking with some people, and expressed interest in working in the broom factory, which I heard, was opening. As luck would have it, one of the men was a *meinster*, and he hired me on the spot, giving me some food stamps, and assigning me to a three-room apartment which I would share with four other girls. For me this was a blessing, because for the first time in many days I had not only a safe place to sleep, but also enough food stamps to get more than the typical meager rations available in the ghetto. It would not be enough food to actually fill me, but at least I wouldn't be starving.

By this time, the ghetto population had dwindled considerably, owing to starvation, disease, and the numerous *aktions*. Most of us left were teenagers and young adults. You saw few children, and no old people. Where apartments full of people had been, now empty buildings stood, except in areas where the buildings had been converted into factory complexes.

In the middle of each complex would stand the factory itself, and the surrounding buildings would house the workers. Each complex would be surrounded by barbed wire. Armed German guards would be watching every movement. Between the complexes would be a sort of no man's land of bombed out skeletons of buildings and empty surviving ones. And here, of course, it was forbidden to go.

At first, I was pleased that I would no longer have to roam the streets in search of food and shelter, and I was hopeful that this place would allow me to survive the war. My hair had become so dirty that I had to cut off my braids. I had sores on my head, which I eventually got rid of by swathing them in strong grease. Had I not been able to do so, I would certainly have been selected for extermination. My job entailed binding brooms together with wire, and since we had no tools I had to do it by hand, which was quite difficult. Our *meinster* was not a mean man, and though he constantly reminded us that we had a quota to fill, he never treated us badly.

In the middle of one workday about a week after I began, SS men appeared accompanied by Ukrainians and Lithuanians in black uniforms. They summoned everyone down into the courtyard, and there, to my surprise and horror, held a *selektion*. Hundreds were marched out and sent to *Umschlagplatz* to be transported to *Treblinka* and other death camps. There was no evident reason why one person was selected and another passed over, but I was lucky many times and was never selected. Now, like the ghetto itself, our workforce was getting smaller and smaller.

One particular day, I stayed behind and hid in the apartment because I had a premonition there was going to be a *selektion*. I heard some children crying outside, and peeked out from the drawn shade, where I saw about ten little children crying. They had apparently had been discovered hiding in the surrounding buildings. A Nazi officer was lifting each one in turn by the hair and shooting them dead. I began crying, and the sight of this incredible inhumanity was so overpowering that it made me vomit as well. This image haunts me to this day. The officer was not a human being, but an animal walking on human legs.

The following day I returned to work, and for a few weeks there was quiet until the *selektions* began again. Something happened to me at this time that I consider one of several miracles over the course of time that saved me.

One day, I was in my apartment when suddenly I heard the whistles and the hollering of the Nazis shouting *"Alles raus!"* (All out!), which marked the beginning of a *selektion*. I was really trapped; there was nowhere to go. I heard them ascending the stairs, so I just walked down. We knew there was a train of cattle cars waiting in *Umschlagplatz* that needed 150 people to fill up each car, and the Nazis were here to get them. There was already a line of people in the street guarded by Nazis in front and back as well as some on the sides with dogs. I remember that it was a bright and sunny day. As we were being marched through no-man's-land, I could swear that I heard my father's voice saying to me, "Escape, my child."

I had no idea how to escape. I looked around at all the guards and dogs, but somehow I listened to my father's voice. As we were passing a burned-out store, I darted from the group, bent on escaping into the store, and several others followed me. As I entered the store, the glare from the sun prevented me from seeing anything, and I just ran as far as I could, stopping only when I ran into something metal. Then I just crouched down and stayed very still. I could hear the Nazis in the store, hollering and exercising their whips to try to locate the people who had escaped. I heard shooting, but I stayed totally still. Again I heard my father's voice, this time telling me to stay and not move. I don't know how long I stayed like that. After a time, it was finally quiet, and I opened my eyes. I saw two dead bodies.

I was amazed. Now that I could see, I realized that I had not really been hiding, but was just lying in a corner in plain sight next to a grain scale. I guess that the same glare, which had blinded me, had blinded the Nazis, preventing them from seeing me.

Leaving the store, I had no idea how to get back to the factory, which I had to do because there was nowhere else to go. If I stayed in no-man's-land I would not be able to survive, as there was no food and no one to help me. I walked to the next burned-out building and was accosted by a gun-bearing man who sought to know who I was and what I was doing. I explained that I had been taken from the broom factory in a *selektion* and had escaped by hiding in a store, and that now I was looking for a way to get back to the broom factory. He offered to show me the way if I would take his daughter, a girl about my age, to the broom factory and convince someone to allow her to work there. I agreed and he took me through burned-out buildings and basements till we came into the broom factory underground.

My roommates had assumed I was gone forever, and were glad to see me when I returned. Then I took my young charge to my *meinster*, and eventually persuaded him to give her an identity card and a job.

Again it was quiet for a while. Then one day it was announced that everyone in the factory was to meet on a certain street. I don't know if this *selektion* was drawn only from the broom factory, or if it included other factories, but there were thousands of people standing in the street. We had brought food, and slept that night on the street. This was one of the biggest *selektion*s that I know of.

Several things happened this time that just broke my heart. As I was standing in line, a beautiful little child came over and with tears asked if she could stay with me. I knew that if she did, I would be sent to the side going to the death camps. I felt so terrible that I began crying too. I knew that there was no way for this child to survive whether I took her or not, and that if she were standing beside me, that we both would be taken. So I just consoled her as best I could, and told her to run to the end of the line and look for her mother. I felt there was no other choice.

Another incident the same day was just as heartbreaking. A man was walking with a woman, and the man carried a knapsack on his back in which he was hiding a baby. The baby moved just when a Nazi was looking toward the knapsack, and the soldier came over and pierced the knapsack with his bayonet, killing the baby. Then he sent the father, with the dead baby, to the side being sent to the death camps.

I wanted to know what has happened to the human race. The Nazis were hunters and murderers, seeking Jews as carnivorous beasts seek their prey. And we became like beasts ourselves because our main concern became to survive another day. We lost a part of our soul. There was no time to think or be gentle. Our overriding concern became how to survive, how not to be killed Yet there were acts of kindness among the Jews toward each other. Some of the things we did during the war would be impossible even to consider doing in normal circumstances.

I want to tell about another miracle, which happened to me. Every one of us who survived did so by miracles and some sort of good luck, and I feel we all had guardian angels. Mine was my father. I saw him often at terrible moments in my life where, rationally, there was no way to survive. It sounds strange, but at these moments I heard my father's voice telling me what to do.

Our apartment in the broom factory complex consisted of two rooms plus a bathroom and a kitchen, which had no window and was thus always quite dark. The large room had a window to the outside and a door set at an angle, which led to the bedroom, which had a window that overlooked the back yard. One day in the winter of 1942, when all five of us girls were lollygaging about in the apartment, we were caught by surprise as a *selektion* began to materialize around us. Not knowing where to hide, fifteen of our teenage friends in the building ran into our apartment, knowing that any minute the Germans would be coming to the door to take us away. These people came to us because I had previously told them about my father telling me from beyond the grave about how to survive. I cried and prayed to G-d and to my father for guidance. At that moment, I saw my father and heard his voice, saying, "My child, hide in the bedroom."

I told everyone, and all agreed there was no other place to hide. We spilled water on the kitchen and large room floor, hoping it might freeze and become an obstacle to anyone wanting to enter. We unscrewed the bulb so it would be dark in the large room. Then we blocked the entrance to the bedroom with a small kitchen cabinet and piled two huge bundles of pillows on top to block the transom. We cut a hole in the back of the cabinet for us to go through into the bedroom to hide and covered the bedroom window with a blanket so we wouldn't be visible from outside. And we prayed.

We sat quietly as we heard shots being fired. We also heard people screaming, and finally the Germans coming into our apartment. I remember them saying, "Those filthy Jews, the house is so dirty." As they were looking around, one of them kicked the kitchen cabinet. G-d was with us because the bundles on top didn't fall. After a short time they left. The building had three floors, and the apartments directly above and below us were the same floor plan as ours, but the Germans apparently didn't notice that our apartment seemed to have one less room. Perhaps they were distracted—I don't know—but it certainly was a miracle.

Everyone sat in the room for the entire day. When we left, the building was empty. We were the only survivors. I lay my head down; possibly I fell asleep, dreaming. Again I heard my father's voice, this time telling me not to stay in this place but to go to the factory. All the people in the room tried to dissuade me. They said I would be killed on the way there since we were not allowed on the street after dark and it was dark already. But I wouldn't listen because my father had told me not to stay here and therefore I had to leave. I packed a small suitcase with my few belongings and walked to the factory. The streets were deserted. I saw no one.

Arriving at the factory, I found an open room and fell asleep in a chair. I awoke as people began to come in to their jobs, and told them what had happened in our building. Everyone began crying. That same day, I learned that the Germans had come back, and had found all nineteen people who had remained in my apartment.

I stayed at the factory for that day, and when I was sure that the *aktion* (police action) was finished, I returned to my apartment, where I found another girl from the factory who had moved in after the others had been taken away. She didn't ask any questions and I didn't offer any explanations. She was from a small town and had moved to Warsaw before the war and then been caught like the rest of us. I remember that she was pretty nice, and we lived together until the uprising.

CHAPTER 10

The Warsaw Ghetto Uprising

Sh'ma Yisrael Adonai Elohaynu Adonai Echad.
Barukh Shem k'vod malkhuto l'olam va-ed.

Hear, Israel, the Lord is our G-d, the Lord is One.
Blessed be the Name of His glorious kingdom
forever and ever.

The uprising was to begin two months later, and the intervening weeks were quiet. The Nazis led us to believe they were treating us better, even allowing us to make *matzos* for the first time. Of course all this time they were preparing to liquidate us. This was the legendary Nazi sadism at work. How can anyone call them human beings?

About this time I joined a small group of young people who were organizing and discussing an uprising. We all swore an oath to die without giving another person's name if the Nazis caught us. The plan included building bunkers, but since knowledge was distributed only on a need-to-know basis, at first I did not know their proposed locations. We talked about how to get food and medical supplies for the bunkers, and some of our people agreed to smuggle themselves out of the ghetto to get ammunition from the Aryan side, and we tried to get money from wherever we could. This was really the birth of the uprising.

Before the war, I had been trained in first aid, so I was designated as a medic. A protocol of secrecy was developed so that the ten members of my group learned his or her job, but little about other members of the group. And even the existence of a medical group was kept secret from the others.

Hitler's birthday was April 20, and the Nazis wanted to give him a Jew-free Warsaw for his birthday. For that reason, we began the uprising on April 19, which just happened to be the first day of Passover. We thought it fitting, however, because Passover is a celebration of freedom from bondage, and we were fighting to overthrow our cruel masters.

The uprising was widespread, encompassing both the larger ghetto and the small one. The broom factory was in the large ghetto; the Tabens and Schultz factories were in others. For this reason I can speak only about what was going on in and around the broom factory. I worked there I was in possession of some knowledge, but others knew a great deal more. Because I was considered trustworthy, one of those who did recruited me to make Molotov cocktails in the basement of my building late at night. This was done by pouring gasoline into our collection of assorted empty bottles and affixing a wick from whatever scraps of material we could muster. Then instead of hiding them, we covered them with a blanket and left them within easy reach on a table.

During the evening of April 18, we learned that SS as well as Latvian and Ukrainian troops backed up by a corps of tanks, had surrounded the entire ghetto. We were told to go down to our assigned bunkers. My roommate wasn't part of our insurgent group, and had not been assigned to a bunker, but when I started to leave she followed me. We realized then that we had no choice but to let her in. To leave her out was to destine her to certain death and ourselves to discovery should she be captured and tortured.

To get into the bunker we went down to a first-floor apartment where, hidden beneath a wide windowsill, was a ladder leading to the basement. In the basement was another ladder, not visible from the top, which led down to the bunker. Considering our limited resources, the bunker was remarkably well constructed and well provisioned. It was stocked with food for thirty people and boasted bunk beds, electricity from the city grid, a fresh water well, a tunnel connected to the city sewer and a chimney to provide fresh air.

When we first began planning the uprising, everyone involved made a pact that we acknowledged that while our chances of survival seemed nil, we still wanted to die with dignity and we wanted history to record that it was not to be that the Jews allowed themselves to be taken like lambs to slaughter. We were prepared to fight to the last person.

The first day of the uprising, the women sat in the bunker and the men wait-ed on the rooftops or on balconies with homemade Molotov cocktails and a few guns for the Nazis. The first German tank that tried to enter the broom factory was promptly blown apart by Molotov cocktails. This surprised the Nazis. They turned and fled. Then we heard them on bullhorns asking us to come out of the bunkers, promising to resettle us to the small town of Trevniki where they said we could work and survive the war. The man speaking, Commander Jurgen Stroop, was the officer in charge of the liquidation. He gave us his word of honor. Our answer was "No." Never again would we allow them to take us to kill us. We would fight to the end.

Every morning, the fighting began with the Nazis pounding the ghetto with artillery shells. They always shot from outside the ghetto with artillery and grenades. At first they seldom entered the ghetto. Our brave boys stood on the rooftops, shooting any German who did come in, and throwing Molotov cock-tails over the wall. Only then, did I discover that we had quite a few bunkers, and that the famous one at Mila 18, command post for the uprising, was close to ours. I later learned that its commander—the hero of the uprising—was Mordecai Anelewicz, a young man I had known in his student days. Our bunker was at Szweintojerska 30, and was in close communication with the command post throughout.

Internal communication was by radio, the telephone system, and by scouts who operated at night when the Germans didn't enter the ghetto. Each night, one or two men from each bunker would convene outdoors to swap information and try to ascertain how the situation. Inside, we would be warned by radio or phone to turn down the lights or to be quiet when the Nazis were known to be close. I even remember one night when a young man with tears in his voice asked us to pray, and remember soon after being told of his having been killed.

The atmosphere in the bunker was heavy with sadness. We were frightened, praying for a miracle, and feeling that these were the last minutes of our lives. Every one of us tried to remember our parents, our dreams, our hopes, and all that we had had before the war. We were certain that one person with the power to destroy us would end it all. It was difficult to imagine that one individual, who looked like a human being but was in actuality a terrible devil, could have this kind of power over the lives and deaths of so many people.

At that moment I questioned G-d. "Where are you, G-d?" I asked. "Why do you allow this to happen? Haven't we suffered enough already? Wasn't it enough to see the hunger, the starvation, the beatings and killings and the streets full of the dead and dying? Do we now have to pay with the only thing we have: our lives? And why, why G-d? Why?" Even after everything I'd been through and seen, I now wanted desperately to survive.

We know that the majority of the Jews in the ghetto were decent people who tried, despite horrible suffering and deprivation, to survive as Jews and as human beings. We know that in the ghetto many risked their lives to aid others and that many, many fell as unnamed heroes. We know that many smuggled food and ammunition to us with the sure knowledge that this could lead to their deaths, but they so believed in the justice of our cause that they were willing to pay with their lives. With sorrow, we also have to acknowledge that there were some who betrayed us, though I have no idea what would motivate a person to act in this manner. I was witness to one of those betrayals.

One night a girl named Sapka, a boy named Mark, and I went out to find out what had been happening that day. Mark had a gun with him for protection. Each day, we had a different password so that we would know who was on our side and who wasn't. Because we knew that there were traitors working for the Nazis, we were supposed to kill anyone we met who didn't know the password. Walking through a building passageway, we came upon a young boy of perhaps seventeen or eighteen who did not know the password. Mark prepared to shoot him, but Sapka and I intervened. His story was that he was looking for his mother, whom he thought was hiding in one of the bunkers. He said he knew he was risking his life, but that he just had to find her.

After convincing Mark not to kill him, we took him into our bunker to keep watch on him, and he stayed for a few days, telling an involved story about how his mother had come to survive when everyone else was taken away. Eventually, we allowed him to leave the bunker to continue his search. He left the bunker at night, and the following day we heard the Nazis trying to open the windowsill to get into the bunker. Some of our people escaped through the tunnel to the sewers, but there wasn't time for everyone to escape. Actually, there was hardly time to think before they were upon us, so we were just waiting for them to come and take us.

First, the Nazis sent in the young boy whom we had saved. One of our guys standing near the entrance recognized him and bit him in the nose. Had there been time, he would have killed him. Hysterical crying filled the air. We didn't know whether we would be killed in the bunker or outside. They threw in tear gas and screamed for us to get out. My eyes were watering; I was sick; we all thought this was the end. I remember saying to myself the *Shema* (a prayer that is a profession of Jewish faith.)

Sh'ma Yisrael Adonai Elohaynu Adonai Echad.

Barukh Shem k'vod malkhuto l'olam va-ed.

Hear, Israel, the Lord is our G-d, the Lord is One.

Blessed be the Name of His glorious kingdom forever and ever.

The next thing I remember was being in another courtyard located in the next building. I have no idea how I got from one courtyard to the other. I know that I was barefoot, but I don't remember how I lost my shoes. I do remember standing in the rubble of a burned out building trying to hide, and that I was not alone. When I think about it now, we seemed like rats trying to hide in a cellar, and certainly this must be how we felt at the time.

We had no idea what the next moment might bring, as we shared what little food we had among us. We came upon another bunker and went in, finding that it was not as well provisioned as ours had been. There was little space and little food, especially for us newcomers. There was no more fuel for Molotov cocktails Sapka and I were among only eight people from our bunker who escaped. This was the beginning of May, some two weeks into the uprising.

The Nazis acknowledged that they were losing many soldiers, certainly more than we were. Of course, we knew that they had far more resources than we—an entire army if necessary—so we knew it was only a matter of time until they would overpower us. But we continued to resist.

By this time the Nazis realized that they would not be able to get us out of the bunkers with their soldiers, so they began burning each and every building in the ghetto. The fire was tremendous; it seemed like the whole world was in flames. Because we got our fresh air from the outside, we knew that eventually the chimney through which we received our air would collapse and we would be overcome by flames and smoke. However, our leader told us to wait until the building burned to the first floor, and then to thoroughly wet ourselves, our clothing, and our hair and to hold a wet cloth to our mouths to keep the smoke from choking us.

Around May 2 or 3, a few days before I was captured, they began burning the broom factory complex. Most of us did as we had been told, and when the fire reached the first floor, we wet ourselves and ran out of the bunker. Rather than be captured, some committed suicide by taking a pill rather than leaving the bunker. A couple of people tried to escape through the sewer system, and were killed in there. We exited into the courtyard of a very large apartment building, we saw an inferno consuming it, much of it already destroyed.

How can I describe this terrible tragedy, this horrible, unbelievable scene? We knew there was no place to hide, knew that we would have been suffocated or burned alive had we stayed in the bunker, and knew that no one was listening to our cries. So we just held our cloths to our mouths, tried to hide as best we could, prayed, and cried, knowing that we needed a miracle to survive.

I saw huge pieces of burning wood falling from the building. One woman had a young baby, a few months old at most. He was lying bundled on a pillow attached to a small board, the way babies were traditionally carried in Europe at this time, covered with a cloth tied for his protection. As she held him, a large fiery piece of wood came flying off the building and fell into the bundle. Everyone began screaming, and the woman was forced to abandon the bundle. I remember that she was half crazy, screaming and crying, knowing that there was nothing she could do to save her baby. It was one of the most horrible things I had to witness. There we were, with no help from either people or G-d.

May 5 dawned sunny, with fires burning all around us, and the smoke thick and stifling. The screaming and praying still rings in my ears. Several of us were trying to hide in a burned out building when the Nazis found us. I walked out with the rest, but even as we were leaving the resistance fighting continued.

The Nazis gathered us all together and took away the men, supposedly to clean the bunkers. About ten of us girls were marched to a wall and told to face it and reach up with our hands. I was certain they meant to kill us. Again, I said the *Shema* and prepared to die. I heard shooting, and after a few minutes heard a command to turn around. They hadn't killed any of us, but were just laughing. For them, this was just a little amusement. Were they really human or just vicious beasts standing on their hind legs?

We were all shocked. I didn't know whether to be thankful to be alive or worried about what they would do next. Then they brought in some men and took us all to the *Umschlagplatz*, whipping us all and killing a few as we went. Then, they put us in a basement.

I was first in line the following morning, May 6 as we were lined up to enter the cattle cars. Laughing sadistically, the SS man who was counting people off walked up and put out his cigarette on my forehead. Thinking I was on my way to death, I felt nothing, no pain at all, but I remember the incident because sixty years later I still bear the scar. This ugly SS man did give me one bit of satisfaction, however. He spotted the young boy who had betrayed our bunker, who was on his way to the train like everyone else. The SS man pulled him out of line, saying, "You are shit for the Jews and you are the same to us," whereupon he killed him on the spot.

CHAPTER 11

Work Camps, Death Camps

Not getting satisfactory answers, a few of the camp officials went to Majdanek to see what could be done. What they learned was that over a three day period, while playing loud music over the loudspeakers, the Nazis had machine gunned everyone in the camp. There were no clothes.

A train of ten to fifteen cattle cars stood waiting, and they stuffed us in, all squeezed together. The air vents were three-quarters closed, so almost no fresh air was coming in, and there was no food, water or hygiene at all. I was lucky to get a place near the door where some of the knots in the wood had fallen out and I could press my nose to an opening. I find it almost impossible to describe the feeling of being locked in that car. To this day, when I hear the chugging and thudding sound of trains rolling along the rails, I'm taken back to that awful time and the noise turns into the words, "We're coming, the end is near, there is no tomorrow, there is no future."

Even though the sun shone brightly outside, for us inside the train all was in darkness. Inside my car people were screaming and crying, praying and cursing, begging for water. As the cars passed slowly through the city, we heard people calling, "Throw us your diamonds and gold, you're going to die anyway." At that moment I didn't believe that G-d would look at this terrible horror and allow it to happen.

I have no idea how long we were in there, but I know that the distance from Warsaw to *Majdanek* is about 300 miles. We traveled for about two days. *Treblinka* camp was about 70 miles from Warsaw, much closer than *Majdanek*, but the Nazis didn't dare send us there. Both were death camps. At the station near Lublin, not far from *Majdanek*, they opened the doors and were waiting for us with dogs and whips. Yelling and screaming, "*Raus, mach snell, farfluchte Juden,*" (Get out, quickly, miserable Jews) they marched us from the station to Majdanek. I don't remember the distance.

We arrived and saw the sign "*Arbeit Macht Frei*" (Work Will Make You Free). The guards separated the men from the women. The women were taken to a huge exhibition hall. They told us to undress and put our clothes neatly in a pile so we would be able to find them after we took a shower, and to stand in a line completely naked. A very small Nazi holding a whip stood between two doors, and I will never forget his ugly face. He gestured with his whip which door each girl should go through. We thought both doors led to real showers, and I went through the door he designated and took a shower. Upon returning to the hall, I realized that many people with whom we had been standing in line were missing. It was then that we realized the other door led to a gas chamber.

They didn't give us our clothes back; everyone got different ones. There were no uniforms; we just got pieces of clothing, whether they fit or not. I got a large shirt, a skirt, a checkered sweater, and a pair of wooden clogs for my feet— certainly someone else's clothing. We were given no underwear, but I was able to fashion a bra and a pair of underpants from part of the shirt. In the pocket of the sweater I found a small red pencil, which I believe was later to save my life on several occasions. Then they walked us to our barracks in Camp Number Five.

Before the war, *Majdanek* was a huge Polish army camp. When the Germans took over, they added a gas chamber and crematorium, which was in use twenty-four hours a day when we arrived. They had surrounded the entire camp with electrified barbed wire. The overall complex was divided into five camps. Camps One and Two contained gentiles: political prisoners, smugglers, homosexuals, gypsies, and those Christians who had tried to help Jews. Camp Three contained Jewish men from all over Europe, and Camp Four contained mostly Jewish men from the Warsaw Ghetto Uprising.

Camp Five was for Jewish women from all over Europe, but mostly those from the Warsaw Ghetto. Between Camps Four and Five was a small camp for women who had been designated for immediate passage to the gas chamber. I remember a day when some beautiful young girls from Salonica appeared in this camp. I knew they would soon be killed, but we couldn't talk to them because they didn't speak Yiddish. The following day they were gone.

How can I describe life in *Majdanek*? The only thing to say is that if there is a hell it can't be as bad as *Majdanek*. Every morning before sunrise, an SS man or woman came into the barracks screaming, "Alles raus" (Everyone out.) In five minutes, we had to be out of the barracks and in formation to be counted. And again every evening. We had few clothes and it was quite cold. Those who could stand in formation did so, and those who could not were taken away on blankets, never to be seen again. In addition, every day there was a *selektion*, where the SS would walk around and choose others at random.

One day, I became ill with dysentery and couldn't stand or walk, and when time came for roll call I was taken out on a blanket. In my sickness I ceased to care, and prayed to die because I could see no way to survive. But someone had to be watching over me, because on this day the man who did the *selektions* didn't show up and I was returned to the barracks. By the time he showed up again I was feeling better and was able to stand again.

It was impossible to survive by yourself, so we tended to find someone to be close to, someone whose shoulder we could cry. My friend was named Paula. She was everything to me: friend, sister, mother, and angel. She fought to bring me coffee and soup when I was ill. She made sure I didn't leave the barracks in the middle of the night, lest I be caught in the light of the marauding searchlights and be killed. Every day, to appear healthier than I really was, I would put color on my cheeks and lips with the little red pencil I mentioned earlier. I shared this pencil with Paula, but no one else. I am convinced that this little red pencil saved our lives many times.

Since this was a death camp, there was no industry. The work consisted of make work, like carrying stones or clods of dirt and grass from one place to another. If you dropped the stone or if the clod fell apart, you were killed.

The SS women were the worst sadists that could exist and there were lots of them. I remember one especially. Her name was Brigitta. She was beautiful, with long blonde tresses, and she rode on a beautiful white horse. She beat people to death with her whip and there wasn't a day that went by when she didn't kill someone. Another we called *Kobilla*, which means horse in Polish, who kicked people till they fell down and died.

But there was also one we called *Mawa Perelca*, or Little Pearl, who was small and completely different from the rest. She didn't force us to do anything. She would tell us to huddle together to keep warm, and would place girls in the four corners of the field to watch for other SS who might happen by. When they came she would begin yelling and cracking her whip, but she really tried to look out for us, keeping us as warm and safe as possible. She told us she was there because the SS threatened to send her son to the Russian front if she wouldn't work at *Majdanek*. She was an amazing person.

The most ridiculous and useless procedure involved marching us to a grassy area defined by wires strung in such a manner that we could neither stand straight, sit nor lie down. We had to pretend to be pulling weeds from the area. Sometimes we had to maintain this cramped posture for five or six hours at a time.

There were no toilets in the whole camp, only kettles under wooden frames. And these were right out in the open. If someone had to relieve herself in the middle of the night, the guard would surely kill her. The person who was charged with carrying the kettles outside the camp to empty them was called the *sheiscommander*, a job that was rotated among us. One night, when it was my turn *Kobilla* was the gate sentry to whom I had to report where I was going and why. When I said there were 20 of us women who were going to dispose of waste, she yelled at me that we weren't women, but shit. She started kicking and hitting me so viciously that I was afraid I was going to faint. The others said things like, "Keep going," "You can do it," and "Don't fall." Somehow I remained upright.

Amazingly, all twenty of us came back alive that night.

I remember one girl who tried to escape. She was caught, and they brought her back and forced the whole camp to watch while they made preparations to hang her. They stood her on a stool while they put a rope around her neck. One SS man said to all around, "Now you will see what happens to anyone who tries to escape. And if one of you does try, we won't hang just that one, but ten more."

I recall her last words, "Girls, hang on, someone has to survive to tell the story. Don't ever forget me. Tell the world what you saw here." And she began to sing *Hatikvah*, the Jewish national anthem. At that moment, one of the SS men kicked the stool out from under her and she was hanged. After hanging her, they made us stand and look at her body for a long time. When we awoke and went to roll call the next morning, the body was gone.

Even a simple roll call was turned into an opportunity for sadism. Sometimes we would be kept standing there for hours, shivering and fearful. The sun might be shining, but not for us.

I really don't remember how we washed ourselves at *Majdanek* or even if we washed at all. I know that I was there approximately five months and I remember only one time when a group of us we taken to the showers by an SS woman. We were each given a piece of greenish soap, different from any soap I'd ever seen before. It had a grainy texture and didn't lather well. Going to the showers, of course, was a very risky business, because we never knew whether they would take us to the real showers or to the gas chamber. But I knew that if I didn't wash or get clean in some way that I would get lesions or some skin disease. And with such a disease, I would certainly be selected for the gas chamber. So I had to take the chance.

Can you imagine our shock when, after the war, we found out that all of the soap in the death camps had been made from the bodies of human beings? As much trauma and horror as we had experienced, it still did not prepare us for this incredible outrage. My group gathered all the soap we could find and buried it in the cemetery, the same as we would have buried a person. The emotion was tremendous. We cried uncontrollably, realizing that any of this soap could have been made from parts of our loved ones. We said a prayer, hoping to give them as much dignity and honor as we could. Thinking about this distresses me to this day.

The camp kitchen was in a small building near the route we followed on the way to the showers. One particular day, a huge hill of bones appeared next to the building. I couldn't be sure what they actually were, but they looked more like human bones than animal bones. In any case, I never went that way again. Seeing these bones gave me a creepy feeling, which comes back whenever I think of them. In fact, as I am writing this I am getting cramps in my stomach. The thought that human bones might be used in cooking was so horrible to me that I have only mentioned it to a very few people through the years. This time our group was taken to the showers to bathe, and no one was taken out of line to be sent to the gas chambers. Luckily, we all returned safely to our barracks, and felt a bit cleaner and a bit better. Unfortunately, we had to dress in our old clothes, which we had worn for weeks, but at least our bodies didn't smell.

After morning roll call, we got a black liquid that was supposed to be coffee, and a chunk of terrible tasting black bread. Before the second roll call we received watery soup in which we sometimes found small pieces of meat floating. I never touched the meat because I wasn't sure where it had come. I think we received another chunk of bread at this time, but I can't recall exactly. This was the sum total of our nutrition for the day, a ration so meager that it barely kept us alive.

Conditions in the barracks were terrible. We slept on wide wooden double-deck bunks with no mattresses, about fifteen people to each section. We had nothing to cover us but very thin blankets, which were not large enough to cover everyone. The bunks were so crowded that if one person wanted to turn, the other fourteen had to turn with her. People died every night. In the morning, the bodies were taken away.

Every minute of every day was a struggle to stay alive. We were tortured mentally and physically. My prayer at this time was that I would be lucky enough to go to sleep and not wake up the next morning. It was at this time that I began to give up. Death was the only way I could see of getting out of *Majdanek*.

One night, we were told to sleep in our clothes, a strange command because we had no other clothes to sleep in except the ones on our back. The guards told us to be completely ready, but for what we had no idea. Nothing happened that night, so the next morning I questioned a Polish *kapo*, who told me what was going on. She said that everyone in our camp had been scheduled to be killed the night before, but that something had happened that curtailed the plan. She had no idea what.

As the next day dawned bright and sunny, we heard an announcement on the loudspeaker calling all women ages fifteen through thirty to a specific barracks. Inside its huge hall, narrow tables were lined up inside each room, behind which sat men called doctors dressed in white coats. We were required to undress and parade naked past them, after which the "doctor" at the end would either keep silent or ask a woman for her number.

Because no one knew why the numbers were being taken, we didn't know if having your number taken was good or bad. Paula was not sure it was a good idea, but I soon figured out that those whose numbers were taken looked healthier than the rest. Paula had some skin problems and her number was not taken, so I undressed and paraded before the men a second time. This time, I gave the doctor Paula's number, knowing that whatever fate awaited us, we would be together. We saw airplanes overhead, and prayed that they were American and would bomb us to end this terrible thing.

The "doctor" *selektion* incident ended without our being told anything, and the horrible life we were enduring went on without further incident for another two or three weeks. Then again the loudspeaker announced that all women whose numbers had been taken should come to the same large barracks. There were hundreds of us, and once again we were made to undress and parade before men in white coats. This time there was only one large table at the end, and on it were the books in which had been recorded the number of each woman. Near the tables were two SS men with whips, who looked at each woman, asked for her number, and sent her to the left or right. We knew this was some kind of *selektion*, but had no idea what fate they had in mind for us. To my great sorrow, Paula and I were separated. I never saw her again.

After this *selektion,* we were put in cattle cars. These were not as crowded as the cars were when I came to *Majdanek*, and the space on top was open instead of closed. We each had a place to sit, and they gave us black coffee and bread with butter. To this day, I can't remember anything ever tasting as good as the coffee and bread. I remember looking around and saying to the other girls, "We're not going to be killed. We're being sent somewhere."

I don't remember how long we were in the cattle cars, but we ended up in a group of concentration camps near the town of *Skarzysko-Kamienne*. Hidden deep in the Polish woods, these camps were denominated A, B, and C. The prisoners at Camp C were working with yellow powder for ammunition. When the workers turned yellow and got ill, they were taken into the forest and shot. The life expectancy in this camp was very short.

Camp B, where I was sent, I was close to Camp C. It was also an ammunition factory, but we didn't have to handle the yellow powder. We worked twelve hours a day, seven days a week, and were given a Sunday off every three weeks. Food was more plentiful here than in *Majdanek*, but there still wasn't enough to stave off hunger pangs. We were fed black ersatz coffee and a piece of bread in the morning and soup in the evening. Once every two weeks we were given a small piece of butter and a bit of jelly. The quality of the bread was much better and the soup was a little thicker than that we had been given a *Majdanek*. We were also each given a small piece of soap—regular soap, not the kind we had used in *Majdanek*.

Camp B was smaller than Camps A and C, and like all the camps, it was surrounded by electrified barbed wire. Our accommodations here were much better than they had been at *Majdanek*. We slept only two to a bunk, and although there were still no mattresses, there was straw to soften the wood. Here, we got blankets, though they were still not enough for the cold. There were showers and individual outdoor toilets. We had roll calls, but unless something unusual happened we never had to stand for hours. Things were much better than in *Majdanek*.

There were no gas chambers or crematoria in Camp B, but every two weeks those who were too sick to work were taken out to the forest and killed. The majority were men, because they did the most difficult jobs, working on large machines where the oil made them sick.

In *Majdanek,* the police had been cruel, sadistic Polish or German *kapos*. The *Skarzysko-Kamienne* police were Jewish, and treated us much more humanely. They were the ones who made the counts and took us to and from the factory, which was deep in the woods outside the camp. Even so, there was no way they could purposely miscount or let anyone escape since the Nazis knew at all times exactly how many people were being transported to and from the factory.

In *Skarzysko-Kamienne,* I was lucky to meet three wonderful girls who became like sisters to me. One was Marisia Malatcka, a girl from Warsaw whose family knew my family. Extremely bright and talented, she had graduated gymnasium in Warsaw, and was like a walking encyclopedia. The other two, whose first names I don't remember, were daughters of a Polish senator named Trutsker.

Some wealthy Jewish families in the town of *Skarzysko-Kamienne* had paid maids and manual laborers to take their places in the camp. Ironically, the people who took their places survived at least for a time, whereas the wealthy families were taken out into the forest and killed *en masse*. These substitutes had a little money, and we found that we could get extra food or money by working for them, doing their share of the menial jobs everyone was assigned in addition to their normal work in the munitions plant. Marisia did laundry. The two sisters cleaned toilets and I mended men's T-shirts.

When we came from *Majdanek,* we brought only the clothes on our backs,

As we arrived at *Skarzysko,* we were promised clothes from a shipment that was due to come soon from *Majdanek.* When the shipment failed to arrive after about four weeks, our camp officials began inquiring as to why.

Not getting satisfactory answers, a few of the officials went to *Majdanek* to see what could be done. What they learned was that over a three day period, while playing loud music over the loudspeakers, the Nazis had machine gunned everyone in the camp. There were no clothes.

A few gentile women from the town worked with us in Camp B, and occasionally one of them would bring us a piece of bread. Realizing how hungry we Jews were, these gentiles risked their lives to smuggle in food for us. One of these women brought me a piece of bread every day, making me luckier than most.

We needed a change of clothes to keep clean and healthy, so I stole eight T-shirts, two for each of us, taking them one at a time. I was sure that death awaited me should I be caught, but fortunately I wasn't. White T-shirts were worn only by men, so to enable us to wear them we dyed them blue with the help of one of the townswomen who smuggled in the dye. Jewish girls from the town brought us underwear, which we hadn't had in a long time. Thus after many months, each of us had something resembling real clothing and underwear. We still didn't have reasonable shoes, so we used paper to insulate our feet from the cold.

In general, the camp was very cold. Having no coal or wood to burn in the stove, we covered ourselves with paper to keep warm. Although the Jewish policemen sold fuel, we had no money, and two girls had recently frozen to death in the barracks. To get money, the four of us put on a show depicting camp life in a comical way, to which we charged admission. It was a rousing success, with even the Jewish policemen coming and enjoying themselves, and a few of the Polish and German soldiers watching from a distance. Making enough to buy wood, we took turns tending the fire and made sure that no one else froze to death.

In the small amount of free time that we had, the four of us laughed and cried and talked about the future, thus rekindling human emotion. Without this, I don't think any of us could have survived the war.

The soap supply was kept in an unlocked cabinet. One night I happened to see one of the girls go into the cabinet and take a piece. In the morning, the Nazi in charge discovered that there was a piece missing and lined us all up outside. He asked the person who took the soap to come forward, but no one did, so he told us that we would stand there all day and all night unless someone took responsibility. After a long time, he counted off every tenth person, and gave each one ten lashes with his whip. Unfortunately I was one of these, and I remember that I couldn't sit for days. But still, I was glad that no one was killed. Although I knew who had taken the soap, I never revealed it to anyone.

I want to describe a very close call I had, a time when I was certain my time had run out. In the ammunition factory, a girl named Margulies and I alternated in twelve-hour shifts on a line making bullet casings. Working down the line from us was a very beautiful girl from Krakow who had a German officer for a lover. One day in checking the finished ammunition, they found ten thousand defective bullets, and traced the defect back to my controller. Taking Margulies and I back to the barracks, they accused us of sabotaging the bullets, which we denied. They told us we should not go back to work, but wait in the barracks till they came back. We knew that when they came back, they would take us to the forest and kill us.

For about a week we were left alone in the barracks, with my three friends and I praying and crying our eyes out. One day, I asked one of the Jewish policemen to take me back to the factory. At first, he said he couldn't but he, finally gave in. I went back to the place in the line where I used to work and found someone else there. I just stood there and cried. A German officer—not an SS but an SD—came along and asked why I was crying, telling me that he had a daughter my age about whom he was very concerned, since his hometown was being bombed. He took me into his office and questioned me as to whether either Margulies or I had committed the sabotage. Again and again I proclaimed our innocence and swore to him that we hadn't done anything wrong. He told me not to worry, that he would investigate the situation and that if I were telling the truth he would make sure we were saved.

For a while it was quiet. I still wasn't working, and I prayed constantly for a miracle. Then one day it happened. I found out that the beautiful girl from Krakow had been killed in the forest. It turned out that she wasn't sabotaging the bullets, but that she simply wasn't doing her job, thinking that because she had a German lover, she didn't have to do anything. Right then I began to believe in G-d again. This was a miracle, and I could hardly believe it had happened. Afterwards, Margulies and I went back to work. Two months later she became sick and was taken out to the forest and killed.

One other incident I remember vividly. The Russian army was coming closer and we were all gathered together to prepare to leave the camp. We were all counted and told that we were being taken to another camp. Again, the sick ones were taken to the forest and killed. One of the SS officers had a Jewish mistress among the girls, also from Krakow and also very beautiful. She had been in an accident and one of her hands was not functioning properly. He told her that he couldn't send her to the new camp because of her hand, and that because of her hand he was supposed to send her to the forest to be killed; but that if she begged him for her life he would allow her to live. She refused to beg and he killed her with a gunshot in the head. And we were all forced to watch this.

The following day, we gathered our meager belongings and were once again put in cattle cars, this time open ones in which we could breathe easier. We were given food—bread and water, I believe—and traveled for a day and a night. Luckily the sun was shining and the weather good, so we weren't too cold. As we left, once again, people from the village lined the sides of the track, yelling, "Throw us whatever you have because they're going to kill you anyway." But they didn't kill us. They sent us to another camp that also manufactured ammunition, this one outside the city of *Czestochowa*.

When we arrived in Czestochowa, we were kept outside the camp in a holding area surrounded by barbed wire, but we could see the camp itself. I was surprised to see that the people looked so different from those I had seen in the Warsaw Ghetto, *Majdanek* and even *Skarzysko-Kamienne*. These people certainly didn't look like the *musselmen* I had seen at the other camps. *Musselmen* were like walking dead, with sallow skin stretched over skeletal bodies, surrounded by an aura physical and mental death. *Musselmen* showed no emotion about anything and seemed to have given up all hope. These people not only looked healthier but also were walking around dressed in street clothes, something I hadn't seen for years.

While we were waiting to be cleared to enter the camp, one of the main *kapos* who was looking us over offered to make me a *kapo*, which I emphatically refused. To me, a *kapo* was someone who did irreparable harm to his fellow Jews for his own benefit, and I would rather have died than done that.

Finally, in the evening, we were let in the camp and lined up for roll call and a guard began calling out different trades, such as shoemaker, tailor, electrician, plumber, and dressmaker. Those who professed to know these trades were taken from the line and sent away. Here, there were no whips. Later, I was to learn that around the city of *Czestochowa* there were three camps—*Warta*, *Czestochowainka*, and *Pelzery*—and that *Pelzery* was considered the best.

Within a few hours, everyone was gone, including my friends Marisia and the two sisters. Now there were only three of us left, and I was not acquainted with either of the other two. To the guard's question as to my trade, I answered that I was a schoolgirl. He replied that since they had no need of schoolgirls here, and then I would be sent elsewhere. Seeing how different this camp was from the others, and knowing that I could survive here, I became frightened that I would be sent away to be killed, and began crying hysterically, asking G-d, "Why, why do I have to die now when I've come to a place where I know it's possible to survive?"

As I stood there, a man walked up and asked why I was crying. This led to a conversation about who I was and the various places I had been during the war. He introduced himself as Arnold Steiner, from *Czestochowa*, and assured me that I would be able to sleep in the barracks there that night. He also told me that in the morning he would see if he could do anything to help me.

That night, I was relieved to find my three new friends in the barracks. They laughed at me and asked why I hadn't just created a trade for myself at roll call. When I responded that I feared not being able to do the work, they called me naive, pointing out that the Germans needed people to work in the munitions plant, not dressmakers or shoemakers.

The following morning, Arnold showed up at the appointed meeting place with another man, *a kapo*. In my mind, of course, *kapos* were to be feared, but Arnold told me that things were different here. This particular *kapo*, who had been Arnold's neighbor in *Czestochowa*, turned out to be nice. Arnold told me that I would be assigned to one of the work groups, but that after roll call every day I should return to the barracks instead of working. I found this unsettling, and asked, "How can I be in a Nazi work camp and not work?" Arnold merely smiled, and said I must trust him. I knew I had no choice, but realized that if he were paying for my safety that I would have to return the favor somehow. He answered that he did not pay, but that the *kapo* did it for him as a gesture of friendship. To my question as to why he did this for me, Arnold answered that I reminded him of his beloved sister, who had been killed.

So I began the regimen of reporting to roll call each day and then returning immediately to the barracks. Because food was distributed at the work place, Arnold brought me food, and eventually started bringing extra food for my three friends. When again I broached the subject of payment, he agreed to keep a written record of my debt, so that I could pay him back if we both survived the war. He also indicated that I wasn't the only one who owed him money. As time went on, we developed a friendship. I asked him to stop calling me "Miss Basia," at which time we began to address each other by our first names.

Over the course of time, I learned that Arnold and his brother were involved in black market activity, smuggling money and commodities, and were doing business with gentile Poles who came in and out of the camp to work. In addition, he was involved with the underground, which was also smuggling money into the camp.

One day, I noticed that a Nazi officer saw me returning to the barracks after roll call, and saw him pointing a finger at me as he spoke to a *kapo*. Somewhat frightened, I reported this to Arnold when he next brought me food. He tried to calm me, saying that this *kapo* had been his best friend in *Czestochowa* and would do nothing to harm me. Unfortunately, he was wrong. That same Nazi officer and *kapo* were waiting for me when I came to roll call the next day. The officer spoke to me in German and I answered in Polish. He then brought over a girl to translate, though I think he knew I understood German. He queried me on where I worked, and I responded by describing the bullet checking section where I had last worked—not knowing it had been closed for some time. He then asked me why I had not worked the day before. With incredible *chutzpah*, I told him I had been sick with a terrible headache and that I had asked the *kapo* if I could go back to the barracks. The *kapo* began screaming that I had never asked him anything and that, in any case, he would not have allowed me to go back.

Again I started to cry, knowing that they would take me to be beaten and that under such pain I might tell about the others who did not work. This frightened me more than the prospect of the beating. I was not afraid of dying, but I didn't want to hurt three other people in the process.

Throughout the war I had survived through a series of miracles, and now another was unfolding. The same Nazi officer sent everyone, including the translator and the *kapo*, back to work. Speaking German, he told me to come with him. Shivering with fear, I followed him, dropping the pretense that I didn't understand. As we walked, we saw the camp commander coming in our direction, and the officer told me to stand still and not to say a word. After exchanging salutes, they each spoke a few words, but nothing about me. As the commander departed, we resumed walking in silence.

We walked into a place filled with Nazi officers relaxing off duty, and it was then that I realized that perhaps he wasn't going to kill me after all. There were many Germans in that room. Now that I think about it, I'm pretty sure he thought it would be empty and that he could have his way with me. He said to them, "You see her? She's been here a year and hasn't done a day's work yet." What a miracle! G-d was with me. None of them touched me. The only thing the officer did was take me over to the factory and assign me simultaneously to take care of three machines. But as everyone knew, it was impossible to look after three machines at once. Risking his life, Arnold continued to bring me food while I was on the night shift. If the Nazis had caught him, surely they would have killed him.

Conditions deteriorated and I soon began to give up. The work was overwhelming and people began falling asleep at their machines because they were so tired and hungry. I also thought that once the Russians were close enough they would blow up the factory and kill us all. I thought we had no chance of survival.

Now every week or so there were *selektions* with no rhyme or reason as to who was being chosen. It seemed that they just chose at random the number needed for each transport. I don't know what happened to them, but I'm confident that most of them died on death marches or in death camps. I was selected several times, but each time I was sent back to the factory. I soon learned that all along Arnold had been paying the Nazi officer to keep me safe in this camp. I just couldn't believe that this man did so much for me and never asked anything in return.

From that minute on, I started to feel what I think was love for Arnold. But remember, when this war began I was a little girl and had no normal experience with boyfriends or love affairs. All this time, I was simply trying to stay alive. I just couldn't believe that this angel had come to save me.

One morning, after working the twelve hour night shift, I returned to the barracks hungry and dead tired, hoping to fall into bed. No sooner did I lie down than I was roughly awakened and told to return to the factory. There, the *kapo* who had been at roll call told me I hadn't cleaned my workstation properly. At this point. I didn't care what he did to me. I yelled, "How could you do this? Couldn't you let me sleep after twelve hours of work? Couldn't you pick up those few little things? What kind of human being are you? You are a Jew and you are a miserable Jew. You are the worst of our people. You are garbage to me. And when this war is over, all the garbage will be thrown away and you'll get your justice then."

As I was yelling, he was hitting me and blood was coming out of my mouth. I lost a tooth that day, but I didn't care any more. After he stopped hitting me, I cleaned up and went back to the barracks. When Arnold saw my swollen face the next day, he was outraged, and said that someday the *kapo* would pay for this.

The *selektions* continued, and in one of the last ones Arnold ran out of money and couldn't pay the *kapo* for both him and me. He paid only for me. He said that he was a man and older, and that it would be easier for him to survive. He then went into hiding within the camp, so they took his brother instead and were going to send him away. When I learned this, I went to the main *kapo* and asked to have my name put on the list as well. He said he wouldn't do that, but I told him I couldn't live with myself knowing that someone who had risked his life and done so much for me would be sent away and I would be saved. I said I had to be able to look in the mirror and would not be able to face myself if I did such an ugly thing. This *kapo* told me to tell Arnold to come to the factory and the *kapo* gave me his word of honor that Arnold would not be sent away. Did I believe him? No, but I felt there was no choice but to do what he said. Arnold came to the factory and, sure enough, he was sent back to work. The *kapo* kept his word.

CHAPTER 12

Liberation

We were free, but where could we go?

I told Arnold that I was giving up, but he insisted that we would survive. He said that his father had come to him in a dream and told him that in two weeks we would be free. Amazingly, exactly two weeks later, on January 15, 1945, Arnold came to me in the factory and told me to come with him, that the Russians were already in the streets of *Czestochowa*. I was afraid because the Nazis were still there and everyone was still at their places working together in the factory. As we left, the Nazis shot at us, but we didn't get hit.

We went to a storage space in the camp and hid. Hitler's picture hung on the wall. Our first act was to remove it and smash it. Our second was to say a prayer of thankfulness that we survived this long and a prayer of supplication that we might leave the camp alive. We were there for many hours, till around midnight when some Jewish people knocked on our doors and yelled that we were free. Everyone was screaming, crying, singing, and kissing. We were free. The Nazis had run away, and the camp was left with some several hundred Jews. Some people took ammunition to kill Nazis. We did not.

Arnold, his brother, Joseph, and I stayed at the camp till the next morning. We went to the Nazis' living quarters and found that they had left in such a hurry that they had left food on the table. Arnold found a ring in the bathroom that someone had left behind. He also found clothes for the three of us to wear, but I didn't want clothes that came from the Nazis, so I walked out of camp in the *shmates* (rags) that I had been wearing when I came to *Czestochowa*.

The morning dawned bright and cold. A Russian tank drove up and told us we were free to go wherever we wanted to, but we had no idea where to go or what to do. It's difficult to explain my feelings upon liberation. This was a moment I'd been dreaming of, praying for, and hoping for, but I didn't really believe that this moment would ever come. I was crying and laughing at the same time. I was looking at people and hoping to find someone familiar to me from my childhood.

We were free, but where could we go? We had no idea what life would be like for us. How could we live and survive as decent human beings, as people who have feelings, when they had been denied to us for so many years? How would we be able to smile? To cry? How would we react to seeing normal tragedies? As a person, would I be able to overcome everything I had seen and been through in these horrible years? Could I ever be the person I was before, raised with feelings and love? Could there ever be a moment when I would be able to care again? I didn't know, and at the time I didn't think there were any answers to these questions.

No one from the Red Cross or any other organization was there to welcome us or make us feel like human beings. In fact, it was the complete opposite. The gentile Poles were saying, "Look at that. They said they killed them all, so where are they coming from?"

We were horrified to hear such talk after everything we had been through.

The war ended and a new chapter of my life began. Arnold, Joseph, and I walked out of the camp together. As soon as we were outside, Arnold said to me, "You know how I feel about you. You know that I love you, but I want you to know that you are not obligated to marry me. You can go back to Warsaw and we could be friends. But I hope that you will marry me and we will begin to have a life together."

Did I love Arnold? This was so complicated. I was just out of hell, liberated, on my own. But what did I feel? I knew that I loved being with Arnold. He was almost like a father figure for me. He took care of me and I felt secure with him. I didn't know my own emotions at the time. If I think about it now, it was love. How could I not love a person who cared and did so much for me, who had taken such risks to save me, who would even have sacrificed his own life for me?

So I said, "Yes." We walked out together and four days later we were married. Not by a rabbi, not in a *shul*, not with the bride in a white gown and veil, not with friends and relatives around us, but simply by a man who happened to know the wedding prayer. Arnold gave me the ring he had found in the Nazis' bathroom, and we were pronounced man and wife. Instead of laughter we hugged each other and cried for hours. That was our wedding day.

Arnold and his brother, Joseph, were from *Czestochowa*, so we headed there and found a building which had been inhabited by Jewish people before the war.

The apartments, which the Nazis had appropriated for themselves, were now empty, and we took two rooms of a large apartment for ourselves. Arnold and Joseph scrounged a table and a bed from other apartments. Then, because they knew the area, they went to a farm whose owner they knew to acquire food. I stayed in the rooms to put things in order.

We had forgotten the basic rules of normal living and, like small children, we had to re-learn how to live independently. We left the bundle of clothes Arnold had bought for me in the camp at the apartment, never thinking to lock the door. When we returned, everything was gone.

Then I tried to cook. I cleaned and cut the potatoes, but because I didn't know better, I put the *farfel* (noodle dough) in the cold water with the potatoes. Instead of soup, I ended up with glue. When Arnold returned, I was sitting and crying, and I told him I didn't know what went wrong, but that this really didn't look like soup. Being hungry, he tasted it anyway, and said, "It's not too bad." He actually ate some of it. I ate only the bread and butter. That was my first experience cooking for my husband as a free, married lady.

A few evenings later, on a particularly cold January night, we were walking near our building when we noticed a Russian soldier shivering near a tank parked in front of our building. When I asked him where he slept, he indicated that no one would let him come into the building. I was outraged. I felt this was so unjust, that the Russians had liberated us and yet no one would let this poor freezing man come inside. I asked Arnold if we could bring him. Of course, he agreed. We made him a pallet of blankets on the floor and shared our food with him. Andrei, as he introduced himself, was very grateful for our hospitality.

Before he left the following morning, Andrei said, "From now on, you are my brother and sister, and I will do everything I can to make you more comfortable." And he kept his promise. A few days later, in the middle of the night, we heard a knock at the door. Not knowing who it might be, we were apprehensive until we heard Andrei's voice saying, "Open, don't worry."

Andrei told Arnold and Joseph to get dressed and come down with him, where—right on the street outside the apartment—they found a truck filled with food, clothing, and a live goat! We were amazed. We asked him what to do with all this and what he wanted in return, to which he answered that he didn't want anything except to feed and clothe us. Of course since there was so much, we shared our good fortune with those around us. Now, for the first time since I left the ghetto, I had real clothes! They were rather big on me, but Arnold was able to take them in and shorten them, and even to make me a bra.

Andrei told us that he was being rotated to the front for about three weeks, and that if he didn't return we would know that he had been killed. Sadly, we never heard from him again. Thus began our post-war life.

PART III

In Search of a Homeland

CHAPTER 13

Displacement in Our Own Land

I just wanted to find anyone I knew who had survived who would know who I was.

The war was finally over in May of 1945. After losing so many of our people to the Germans, gentile Poles continued to slaughter Jews. One of these casualties was a cousin of Arnold's who had survived both the war and the camps. Upon returning to the *Czestochowa* area to reclaim a farm that had belonged to his parents, he was killed by Polish peasants. Such killing went on for some time. So did organized pogroms such as the one in *Kielce* as late as 1946, in which some 46 people were killed.

After the war. Arnold went back to his old trade of curing leather. He was quite successful, bringing in a good amount of money. But in Poland, we were subject to a Russian occupation. The communists were starting to curtail private ownership.

One day I read in the newspaper that anyone caught curing leather would be sent to prison for five years. So we moved to Neidershlazen, a part of Germany that had been annexed by Poland after the war, to a city called Reichenbach by the Germans, *Dzierzonow* by the Polish. There we took over a business, and again became quite successful.

Though we had become comfortable materially, I still suffered great emotional distress from my feelings of guilt. I sought relief from many rabbis and doctors. Each tried to convince me that I should feel no guilt because of my family's deaths, but no one could erase the feeling from my mind and heart. When the trains began running again, we decided to travel to Warsaw in search of my oldest brother, hoping at least to find some members of our large family or friends. Actually, I just wanted to find anyone I knew who had survived who would know who I was.

I returned to my family's old neighborhood, and found that their building had been destroyed. I went to relatives' and friends' houses, and found no one. I went to the Red Cross and the Jewish Committee, and scoured the areas where the Jewish businesses had been. I found no one. Nothing was left. Everything was destroyed. Everything was gone. I couldn't find even one person who had known me before the war. I began to give up. I nearly collapsed. I started asking myself, "Why did I survive? Was I stronger than my older brother, or my aunts, my uncles, and my cousins? Was I somehow better than them? Why me?" All these gentle, wonderful people: dead. I thought back to walking over the dead bodies. I had experienced so much horror, known about the gas chambers and crematoriums, and yet I had survived. Why, and for what? With the best of our people gone, I felt life was not worth living.

After returning to Reichenbach with Arnold, I was a broken person, consumed with survivor's guilt, not willing to live. I took an overdose of pills, but Arnold caught me and took me to the hospital where my stomach was pumped. He asked me why I did it, to which I replied that I had no right to live when all the others were gone. A few days later I came home, still terribly depressed and blaming myself for things I hadn't done for my mother and brother while they were still alive. I knew logically that I couldn't have saved them, but I was so ashamed of my behavior that I couldn't stop thinking about it. Arnold took me to a doctor.

Later, I tried suicide again. I was about to jump from a third-floor window when Arnold caught up with me and pulled me back. The doctor told Arnold that he was sure I would try again, and suggested that the only thing that could save me was getting pregnant. I was so depressed that I didn't want to even think about getting pregnant, but soon I was. The draft was still in effect and Arnold was draft age, so I was also afraid he might be taken from me, and had no idea how I would cope alone with a baby to care for. So I found a doctor who would give me an abortion. It was done in a hospital, so everything was clean. When he found out, Arnold was very upset. My thoughts were so turbulent that I really didn't know how I felt.

Some time later, in 1947, I had an amazing dream. In it, I saw my father in *shul* dressed in a *kittel* with his best *talis*, blowing *shofar*. I was sitting in the balcony with my mother. My father called me down, hugged me and covered me with the *talis*, kissing my forehead. He said to me, "My child, you will have a son; name him after me." I woke up screaming, and woke Arnold as well. I told him I was pregnant again and that I was going to have a son. He was mystified and thought I was hallucinating. I went to the doctor and sure enough, I was pregnant. This time, I wanted the child very much.

I was sure that I was carrying a boy, to be named after my father. I delivered at a Catholic hospital, and was anaesthetized, as was the practice at the time. When I awoke the doctor asked me if I would like to know the sex of my child, to which I replied, "I already know; I had a boy." At that, the doctor gasped, crossed himself, and asked, "How could you know? How did you know?" And I explained that I knew I was carrying my father's namesake. My son, Moshe Peretz Steiner, named after my father, Moshe, and Arnold's father, Peretz, was born on September 3, 1948. In English, we called him Marvin Paul. He shares my father's love of learning in general and the study of languages and religious subjects in particular. He grew up to become a physician specializing in internal medicine.

From that time on, I never again saw my father in my dreams.

CHAPTER 14

Emigration to Israel

*In 1947, I had an amazing dream. In the dream,
I saw my father in shul dressed in a kittel with his
best talis, blowing shofar.*

While I was pregnant with Marvin, I began to think about what I was qualified to do in the world with so little education. Before the war, I had gotten a good education at private schools, which had enabled me to tutor during the war. Not having even a high school diploma, I decided to go back to school. I found one designed especially for people like me whom the war had prevented from completing their educations. In two years I got a high school diploma with a certificate in bookkeeping, which was to prove of enormous help in the future.

In Reichenbach, Arnold and I owned a successful clothing business. We had everything we needed materially. Marvin was a wonderful little boy on whom we doted constantly and life was very pleasant. The horror of the war, however, was never far away. Both of us had horrible recurrent nightmares of Nazis chasing us and having no place to hide. We would wake up from these screaming and in cold sweats. Thank G-d we were there to comfort each other. We'd talk about our situation and about the people we'd lost. We'd each lost so many. And there were always one or two who had been so special to us that we'd talk about them at length. We had to talk, for there was nothing else we could do, except cry. Eventually, we would go back to sleep, but these nightmares came often. For me, these deep fears continue to this day, not as often as before, but still the same nightmares and feelings surface from time to time.

We were aware and saddened by the thought that our child would never have the privilege and happiness of knowing his grandparents, uncles, aunts, and cousins.

Along with this, we were living in Poland, now a communist country, where there was no real individual, personal freedom. We were desperate to leave. We were afraid that if anyone denounced us for any reason, we would end up in jail. An individual who has ever resided in a communist country will understand this completely. Yet we couldn't leave Poland for two reasons: exit visas were not available, and, even had they been, no country wanted to let Jews in. Since it was prior to 1948, there was no Jewish state of Israel. The communists were gradually confiscating all private businesses, and it was only a matter of time before they got to ours.

In 1949, the Polish government announced that Jews with entrance visas for Israel would be allowed to emigrate. The next year the Israeli government began issuing such visas to Polish Jews who had relatives already in Israel. Arnold and Joseph went to Warsaw to seek Israeli visas for us. Arnold was meticulous about his appearance, but Joseph didn't pay much attention to his. Because the Israelis were seeking people who could do hard manual labor, Joseph was given a visa whereas Arnold came away empty handed.

We were very upset and decided that I should give it a try. Arriving at the Israeli Embassy in Warsaw, I was confronted by a huge line of visa seekers snaking around the building. Quickly realizing that all the visas would have been given out before I could reach the head of the line, I decided upon a desperate maneuver. Approaching a policeman standing near the line, I gave him my card, telling him that although the man issuing the visas didn't know me, I was bringing greetings and information from his family. Sure enough, I was soon standing in front of the man I sought to speak to.

Bursting into tears and apologizing, I immediately admitted that I had lied in order to be able speak to him about getting a visa. I told him my entire family and my husband's were killed by the Nazis, and that I didn't believe it was right that we now be victimized a second time. I described some of what had befallen Arnold and me during the Holocaust, and in the end, he and I were both crying. He asked me for all of our names, wrote something in Hebrew which I didn't understand, gave it to me, and asked me to leave the office. Returning home, I didn't know whether I had a visa or a shopping list, because I had no idea what was written on the paper. Though Arnold and I both read Hebrew, we couldn't decipher it. We took it to a rabbi and he told us that we all had entry visas for Israel.

I couldn't believe it. I was flabbergasted, amazed, stunned to think that I had really pulled this off. I had not expected my ruse to work. And of course it worked only because of the kindness and understanding of the official in the embassy. I am forever thankful to him for this kindly act.

Before we left, we were required to give up our Polish citizenship. We never told anyone we were leaving because we were afraid that someone would try to stop us. One day in early 1950, we just left our business and never came back. Close to the Czech border, on the train leaving Reichenbach, a Polish official walked through the car calling our names. We did not know for certain why and we were afraid to find out. We sat quietly until we passed the border and no one discovered us. We were thankful to leave the land of our birth, a land that, to us, had become a Jewish cemetery. I knew I would never go back there because every stone, every street, was soaked with Jewish blood.

In March 1950, we traveled by train into Italy, from which we took a ship that arrived at Haifa Harbor in Israel a week later. Just seeing the land and knowing it was Israel made me think about what could have been if we'd had this land before the war.

I was laughing and crying at the same time when we arrived. I was with my people now, people who would take us in and treat us as brothers. From now on, I was in control of my life. No one could tell me where to go or what to do, or treat me as if I were not a human being. Never again would I have to be spoken of the demeaning word *zhid*.

At that time Israel was overwhelmed with people immigrating from all over Europe. So upon arrival, we found ourselves placed in a refugee camp. Aside from needing to guard against the introduction of infectious diseases, the Israelis literally didn't have places to house everyone who was coming. One can imagine how difficult is was for such a small country to absorb approximately twice its present population. It was an incredible feat, yet this was exactly what happened.

Arnold, the baby, and I were among the lucky ones. We had managed to contact our relatives before we got to Israel. My uncle Feivel, who had left Poland in 1938, now lived with his family in Rehovot. My cousin Shvalbum, who had been born in Israel, was living in Haifa. Seeing Feivel was very emotional as this was the first time since the war that I had found someone who had actually known me before it. This was a very special moment for me because he was someone who knew that I had had a decent family life in Poland. Soon after we arrived, both Feivel and Shvalbum came to the camp and arranged for us to leave. They took us to a small but adequate apartment in Shunat Ephraim, a small neighborhood outside of Rehovot, where we set up housekeeping. Because of Israel's severe housing shortage, we considered ourselves lucky.

Unfortunately, there was little work to be had in Israel at this time, which was rough on everyone. There was rationing and it was all but impossible to get milk, butter, chicken, and sugar. The only thing plentiful was bread. Luckily, we had surreptitiously sent most of our belongings to Israel before leaving Poland. Now, once more, we were forced to sell some of our prize possessions to buy food. I remember selling my Rosenthal china service for twelve for a chicken and some milk. Crystal, silver—all of it—went to provide sustenance.

I learned then that when I was a young child that my mother's parents had left Poland for Israel, called at the time Palestine. My grandfather was a rabbi, and because they were religious people, their dream was to live and die in Israel. I don't remember either of them, but I did know that they had purchased land in B'nai Brak. So shortly after we moved into or apartment, Arnold went to that city to discover what had happened to them.

Arnold found out that they had been very generous people and that the orphanage there had been named after my grandfather. He also learned that they had left a small piece of land with a little house on it. The mayor of the town told Arnold that the main rabbi of Lod, Rabbi Kutner, was a first cousin of mine whom I had never met. Rabbi Kutner was the oldest cousin in the family and I was the youngest. Before the war he had moved to Rumania and married a lady there. With the outbreak of war they were sent to Russia, and spent the war in Siberia. Shortly after the end of the war he came to Israel, became Chief Rabbi of Lod, and eventually became a teacher of Rabbi Lau, who is currently the Chief Ashkenazi Rabbi of Israel.

When we met Rabbi Kutner, he was thrilled to see me and to know that someone else in the family had also survived. Upon learning that Arnold and I had not been married in a religious service, he remarried us, blessed us, and even wrote a *ketubah* for us. We decided to see the land and house with him and split the proceeds with him. These turned out to be the value of about ten chickens. When I think of what that land is worth today, I have to laugh. We could have been very rich, but at the time we were hungry and in need of any money we could get.

A little later I met another cousin named David Zyskind, my Uncle Nathan's son. He was head of a *kibbutz* near the Syrian border and wanted us to come and live with him there. Not wanting to live in a *kibbutz*, we declined and he was very disappointed. The whole time we were in Israel, I saw him and his family only twice.

Arnold was able to get a few temporary jobs. In the two and a half years we spent in Israel, he worked altogether only about a month.

Arnold's dream was to move to the United States in order to be reunited with two of his brothers who had gone there long before the war. In due time, he received the affidavits that permitted us to move there. For us, this was a time of mixed emotions. Arnold wanted to go, but I wanted to stay. I felt that Israel was my land, my home, the place where I should raise my child. So it was with great sadness that I left Israel in October 1952 bound for Greece, from which we would take a ship for the United States. By the time we entered New York harbor and I saw the Statue of Liberty, I began to feel a little better about leaving. I knew then that I was in a free country where we could have a chance to prosper and live in peace without fear.

CHAPTER 15

Finding a Home in the United States

I tried to tell my Aunt Helen what had happened to me and how her own mother and the rest of her family had been killed. She didn't want to listen; she told me to forget the past and build a new life.

When we arrived in New York City, my Aunt Helen and Cousin Miriam were there to greet us. I had never met either, and we had a week to get to know them before leaving for Chicago.

We expected Arnold's brothers to meet us at the train in Chicago, but no one was there. Finally, from an address we had been sent, we located Arnold's nephew, and through him, Arnold's brother, Irving. The latter had procured a room for us in a small house nearby, and his brother, Arthur, came to see us the next day. Neither brother seemed very happy about our arrival, and now I was very upset that we had left Israel. Over the years we had sent Irving a considerable sum of money from our business in Poland, and it turned out that the money seemed to have vanished into thin air.

So our introduction to Chicago was really unsettling. We ended up having to leave the small room and slept in a park for three nights, at which time Marvin became ill. We took him to a hospital and the doctor wanted to admit him, but I couldn't let him stay there with strangers. Being desperate, I just went up and down the streets ringing doorbells and asking for lodging in return for work. Finally, an old woman let us in, fed us, and let us stay for the night. The next day, Arnold went to the Jewish Federation and learned about a job pressing clothes at

Hart Shaffner & Marx, where he got hired. We ended up staying with this kind woman for about two months, until we could save $100 and rent a place of our own, a beautiful but unfurnished two-bedroom apartment on Avers Avenue near Fifteenth Street on Chicago's West Side. Several months later, after we had saved another $50, I went to the Salvation Army, explained that I had no furniture at all, and was able to get enough furniture to furnish the whole place—living room, dining room, two bedrooms, and the kitchen. To this day, I donate money and other things to this fine charity, which was there for us in our time of need.

Because at $60 the rent on our new apartment was more than we could afford, we took in a boarder who paid $30, and this helped us pay our bills. But just as our burdens were easing a little, Arnold developed kidney stones. He had left home feeling fine, and I was surprised to receive a phone call that he was in the hospital. He passed the stones, but the stress of all that had been happening plus this sudden illness caused him to have a nervous breakdown. He just wasn't the same person he had been before. He had been a happy-go-lucky guy, and now suddenly he had become a hypochondriac. He thought he had cancer and was dying. I knew he was physically fine, but I didn't know what to do to help him.

One day in the middle of the winter, Marvin wanted to go downstairs to play in the snow. This was the first time he'd ever seen snow, and he was intrigued. I felt so badly and cried when I told him he couldn't play in the snow because his shoes were torn. I don't have to describe my sadness as a mother who had to deny her child even the simplest pleasure. Marvin also started to cry, and went to his father, saying, "You're not sick. Mommy said so. You just don't want to work. And because you won't work, I don't have any shoes and I can't play in the snow." When Arnold heard this he started crying, and the next day he decided to go back to work. The child had saved Arnold's life.

Even though Arnold went back to work, I felt I needed to continue working to make ends meet. I knew a little English from the classes I'd taken when I first arrived, but not enough to get a good office job. While Arnold was still home sick, I had worked two jobs simultaneously, days in a candy store and nights in a rubber factory. In the candy store I worked eight hours a day filling bags with candy as it came sliding down a chute. If I didn't have a bag there in time, the candy would fall all over the place. In the rubber factory, I cut large sheets of rubber into smaller pieces, and I still have scars to prove it.

About two months after Arnold returned to his job at Hart Schaffner & Marx I was coming home about three in the morning when I heard someone following me. I began running and luckily made it home, but the incident frightened me so badly that I became afraid to come home by myself at such late hours. For this reason, I began to look for a day job, and we put Marvin in the Arie Crown Day School so that we could both work days.

Although I was attending night school, I still thought my English was too broken to qualify me for an office job, so I looked for factory employment. Walking around in the vicinity of Homan Avenue, I came upon the Sears complex. Thinking the buildings to be a factory, I approached it. A guard directed me to the employment office, where I was given an application which, to my initial consternation, was entirely in English. To my good fortune, however, I happened to sit next to a Polish girl who translated everything I couldn't understand.

The catalog accounting supervisor, a Mr. Gorsica, came over to me, looked over my application, and told me how pleased he was to meet a fellow Pole from Warsaw. However, probably because my maiden name was Zyskind, he suspected that I might be Jewish. It being illegal to inquire into an applicant's religious beliefs, so he asked me whether I spoke Hebrew or Yiddish. Having been warned about such discriminatory tactics, I replied that I did not. He hired me on the spot as a bookkeeper in his department, telling me that to retain employment I must get my high school equivalency diploma within two years. I loved this job; I was making good money, and was proud to be working in an office.

I kept the job for seven years, always taking off *Rosh Hashanah* and *Yom Kippur*, by using vacation days or sick days, rather than indicating my real reason. Being the only Jew in the department, and because these holidays fell on different calendar days each year, no one noticed. Eventually, however, I felt that I needed to level with Mr. Gorsica, so I called him over and told him I wouldn't be in the following day. When he asked why, I told him it was a Jewish holiday. He recalled that when he had hired me he had inquired as to whether I spoke Hebrew or Yiddish. I replied that not speaking them did not mean that I was not Jewish. When I returned from the holiday, he called me into his office and fired me, saying that it was because work was slowing down, which I knew was not true.

When I was notified that I had been denied unemployment compensation, I went to the state employment office to ascertain why, and was given a hearing at which I explained how I had hidden my Jewishness at first and then been fired when I revealed it. Shortly afterwards, I received full compensation. Some time later, I received a letter from Sears, which I threw away, unopened, and sometime after that I received a telegram asking me to come back to work. When I called, I asked for Mr. Gorsica, and was told he didn't work there anymore. I was then transferred to the new supervisor, who asked me to come back. Arnold and I had purchased a laundromat, in which I was needed, so I couldn't accept his invitation. I regretted not being able to return to Sears, as I had really enjoyed the job.

With the help of the $3,000 profit-sharing distribution I got when I left Sears, we made the down payment on a two-flat near the laundromat. One of the apartments was in pristine condition and the other took Arnold and I many hours of cleaning, painting, and installing new flooring before it was livable.

After three years of disappointing profits we decided to sell the laundromat. Pricing it at $7,000, we took a $500 earnest money deposit from a man who said he would return shortly with the remainder. We were amazed that someone had offered full price, because we considered its value to be much less. We could hardly wait for him to return.

At the time he came by the next day, I was alone. He remarked that I looked like a nice lady, and asked if I would tell him the truth about whether he could make a living there, adding that he had five children. I knew that my self-interest required me to say, "Yes, of course," but I just couldn't lie to him. Instead, I blurted out, "This place is not for you," and ripped up his $500 check. Arnold almost killed me for doing this, but I just couldn't have lived with myself had I deceived this poor man. In the end, we gave the business away for $500.

I know it sounds crazy, but we took that $500 and went on vacation, although Arnold went against his will. He thought I was out of my mind, but I felt we needed to rest and restore ourselves. We were still young, and if we could come back from vacation healthy, we would have a much better chance of finding something and would certainly be in a better frame of mind. When we returned, Arnold was able to find a job in a textile factory, where he subsequently worked for many years. I went to see job counselors at the Jewish Federation, and they suggested I look at Baron's, a clothing chain with stores nationwide, but surprisingly none in Chicago. The main office was here, however, and I was hired as an assistant buyer. My job involved working with the buyer to determine the appropriate blouse and lingerie inventory for each store around the nation. I was responsible for initiating the inventory transfers and keeping detailed records on all such transactions, which was quite a bit of responsibility. I loved the job, and dreamed of becoming a buyer myself someday. However, G-d had a different plan for me.

After Marvin was born, we hadn't thought about having more children because our life seemed so precarious. My 1954 pregnancy had ended in a miscarriage, and it wasn't until 1961 that I found myself pregnant again, which came as a wonderful surprise. Muriel Felicia was born on March 10, 1962, and I was thrilled. But since I believed so strongly that a mother should be home to raise her children, this meant that I had to give up my job. When Muriel was seven, I went back to work, this time as a bookkeeper for a high-rise apartment building on Sheridan Road on the North Side. The tenants were very nice to me, and every Christmas I would get a carload of presents. I really liked this job.

One time I had to transact some business on the 41st floor, and then took the stairs up one flight. When the 42nd floor door wouldn't open, I thought it must be because it was the penthouse, and went back down to 41 to get back in to wait for the elevator. My heart sank when it wouldn't open either, and I realized that a key was needed for every floor. The stairs were narrow and the lighting dim, and not a soul was there, but I had no choice but to walk down, and when I finally reached the bottom, a guard standing just outside the unlocked door looked surprised, crossed himself, and said, "Where did you come from." When I saw him cross himself, I realized it was even worse than I had feared. When I told him how I happened to be there, he added, "You are very lucky, because if something had happened to you, no one would have found you for two weeks. They clean this stairwell only once every two weeks.

I enjoyed this work, and in order to advance my career took several accounting courses and other classes. This was an exciting experience for me. The Nazi discrimination against Jews had prevented me from obtaining much of an education as a young person, and I had always wanted to go back to school. I have always felt that you're never too young or too old to learn.

Life was good and things were going well, but we can never escape the past. While reading the newspaper one day in 1972, I came across an appeal for witnesses who had been imprisoned in *Majdanek*. It seems that they had caught some Nazis and wanted to prosecute them. I called the number of the German consulate that was in the advertisement,. The staff there told me to contact the Jewish Federation, who arranged for everything—flights to Dusseldorf, Germany, hotel rooms, meals, etc. I don't have to tell you how emotional I became upon hearing that among of the camp guards discovered, were Brigitta, the devil in human form; Kobilla, who was not much better; and Perelca, who was like a pearl in that horrible place.

Upon seeing these women, I visualized and lived through everything once again. Being able to point them out and testify against them was the happiest of moments for me. Living to do this for all the people who were slaughtered and could therefore no longer speak for themselves was a great victory for me.

I remember testifying against Kobilla, who denied us the least shred of humanity. Receiving the judge's permission to address her in German, I stepped very close to her and said, "Do you remember when I said to you that twenty women would be disposing of waste, and you said to me that we weren't women, that we were garbage, that we were shit? And then you beat me?"

With tears in my eyes, I said to her, "You are the one. I survived, and now it's time for you to pay for all your sins and all the horror you caused every one of us in that hell. You are what you called me. You are the garbage; you are the shit. After this I broke down in hysterical crying and had to be removed from the courtroom. I couldn't testify any more that day, and had to return the next. Upon returning, I testified against Brigitta, that most terrible sadist, riding on her white horse and killing people. The guard we called Perelca was like a little pearl for us, truly a good person. She protected us and took chances to save us and keep us alive as much as was possible for her. Kobilla and Brigitta got life in prison. Perelca was freed.

Although life had been going well, and although thoughts of the war were never far beneath the surface, going back to Germany to testify had brought everything back to the forefront. When I returned to Chicago, it took me some time to get back to normal everyday life with its workaday responsibilities.

A few years later, in 1976, a movie about the "The Holocaust" came out and changed the lives of Holocaust survivors in America by altering the American public's perception of the atrocities experienced by Jews in Nazi Germany. Now, for the first time, American Jews were interested in hearing our stories. I remember that when we first came here, I tried to tell my Aunt Helen what had happened to me and how her own mother and the rest of her family had been killed.

She didn't want to listen; she told me to forget the past and build a new life. I don't think she ever let me tell her about her own family in Warsaw. We survivors needed someone to tell and shoulders to cry on, but no one was interested.

In 1977, a small group of neo-Nazis announced their intention of marching through the streets of our village of Skokie, a suburb just north of Chicago. It is a community that is home to many Holocaust survivors, including Arnold and myself among them. The rabbis told us to ignore the Nazis, to pay no attention. But we survivors could not accept this. We knew that never again would we shut the windows and pull down the shades.

This time we would fight back. We would not allow them to march. Thanks to our mayor, Albert Smith of blessed memory, we joined together. Most of the community, including both young and old Jews, gentiles and all of us Holocaust survivors stood up to make sure that the Nazis would not intimidate anyone physically or mentally. Eventually, because of our efforts, the Nazis decided to march elsewhere, even though they had legal permission to march in Skokie. It's a good bet that the knowledge that all these people—some outraged and armed with baseball bats—were waiting for them in Skokie convinced them to publicize their evil ideas and intentions elsewhere.

After this event, I joined a group of twelve to fifteen Holocaust survivors who gathered to discuss what had happened. We realized that the people in this country didn't know much about the Holocaust, about how it began and what actually happened. We came to realize that it was our mission to educate the young and old about the Holocaust and to counteract hatred with education. Thus was born the Holocaust Foundation of Illinois, and since then, through hard work, persistence, and determination we have achieved more than we ever dreamed possible; from this small beginning building a foundation with thousands of members. We now have our own building, a museum of artifacts and pictures, docents, a speakers' bureau staffed by survivors, and an impressive staff of dedicated educators who offer classes for teachers.

To date, tens of thousands of students have come to the foundation to tour the museum and hear survivors speak. We also send speakers to schools, churches, and fraternal organizations in Illinois and elsewhere. Under the leadership of our extraordinary past president, the late Erna Gans, we helped make Illinois the first state to mandate Holocaust education in all public schools. Illinois parochial schools, though not required by law to participate, have also decided to provide

Holocaust education. Catholic educators have been some of our most vociferous advocates. I am proud to be a founding member of the Holocaust Foundation of Illinois, now over 25 years old, and am thankful that we have been so successful. In these difficult times, our children need knowledge and guidance to counteract the evils they face, and I am grateful to be part of an organization which spreads light, understanding, and love.

Our Children's Lives Go On

From the moment we arrived in this country, we knew that the opportunity and freedom the United States offered were very important for our children as well as for Arnold and me. We knew that no other country could provide this for us. We really denied ourselves for the children's benefit, because the most important thing for us was to see them thrive and grow up as typical Americans. Because we had lost so many in our families, we put all of our hopes and dreams into our children. We provided our son and daughter with the most that we could materially, but above all, we gave them all our love and tried to open the treasures of our city to them. We took them to concerts, museums, the zoo and any other free educational exhibits we could find.

Time was flying and our children were growing up. Our son, Marvin, an excellent student, who had dreamed of becoming a doctor since early childhood, was accepted at Chicago Medical School after graduating from the University of Illinois with degrees in biology and chemistry. In his last year of medical school he married his high school sweetheart, Eva Solomon. Upon graduation from medical school in 1976, he did his internship at Cook County Hospital and a residency in internal medicine in Peoria, before entering practice in Flossmoor, a suburb south of Chicago.

Our daughter, Muriel, an exceptionally bright child who loved to read and play the piano, was a National Merit Finalist, and although courted by many colleges, chose the University of Illinois in Champaign-Urbana. However, because she knew it would be very difficult financially for us to send her away to school at that time, she decided to attend the University of Illinois at Chicago. Upon becoming aware of this, however Marvin and Eva indicated that they felt so strongly that Muriel should be able to go away to school that they paid for her entire college and graduate school education. Most important, neither Muriel nor Arnold and I were ever made to feel uncomfortable about this. Arnold and I are very proud of Marvin and Eva both for their generosity of both money and spirit.

Upon graduation, Muriel joined the psychology department at Swedish Covenant Hospital in Chicago. In 1990, she met a young man named Scott Blumstein and immediately told me that she knew she was going to marry him the first time she had spoken to him on the phone. I understand that his feeling was the same. I thought they were crazy, but on June 6, 1992, they were married.

Not only were Marvin and Eva generous with Muriel but also with Arnold and me. We had mentioned that we saw a lovely condominium while vacationing in Florida, and they bought it for us. In fact, I still spend the winter there every year.

About this time Arnold begin experiencing trouble with his heart and wasn't feeling well. He experienced heart failure several times, but he took his medicine and kept going. I tried to take him around to different places and keep him busy, but I knew that he was ill. Muriel and I had both been afraid that with Arnold's illness he might not live to walk her to the *chupah* (bridal canopy). But G-d was good to us and he lived not only for that but to know Marvin's two boys, Aaron and Jonathan, and Muriel's first child, Robie. Unfortunately, however, he didn't live to see Muriel's little girl, Allie.

Arnold died on February 20, 1997. When he went, I felt like half of me died. I always had not only a husband, but also a friend with whom to share joys and sorrows. Now I feel empty and alone. It doesn't make any difference how busy I am all day, At the end of it I'm by myself and that is when I miss him the most. We were married fifty-two years and I have to thank G-d that we were together for that long.

About one year after Arnold's death, we dedicated a plaque in his memory at the Holocaust Foundation. Muriel was unable to attend, but sent us a lovely tribute to her father. I read it at the dedication ceremony, and there wasn't a dry eye in the room.

But life goes on. I am blessed with wonderful children and grandchildren and friends and a have an active life. I still do a lot of work for the synagogue, and I continue as a speaker for the Holocaust Foundation, where I tell my story to young people from all over the Midwest. When I'm in Florida, I speak there as well. It is very difficult for me to tell my story over and over again, but I feel it is my obligation to speak for all my loved ones whom I lost and for all six million innocent Jews and millions of others who perished at the hands of the Nazis.

I want to say just a few words about this wonderful country of ours where I've lived for fifty years. This is the most wonderful country in the world. The United States has given me the most beautiful years of my life, not to mention a good life for my children and grandchildren. Only people like me, a person whose youth and family were stolen by the terrible catastrophe of the Holocaust, can appreciate what this country means to young and old alike and how it stands as a beacon of freedom for the oppressed. May G-d bless this country and all good people who live here.

I hope that my story will in some way help young people realize what prejudice and hatred and inhuman behavior can do. I hope this will inspire them to create a better world for themselves and for the generations to come.

Barbara's Fiftieth Anniversary Address

Arnold and I were blessed to celebrate fifty years of marriage. On that occasion our children gave us a beautiful party, and I would like to include here my remarks on that day.

Arnold and I want to thank you for coming to celebrate with us on our fiftieth anniversary, which is celebrating not only fifty years of our lives spent together, but also the fiftieth anniversary of our liberation from a concentration camp. We are the lucky ones, for having survived the greatest atrocity in the history of mankind.

We survived, but almost everyone else in each of our families perished. We survived, but the memories of the Holocaust and the losses of our loved ones stay with is and will remain with us for the rest of our lives. In spite of that, we started a new life. It was not easy, but we made it.

After three years we had our son, and one year later we left Poland, which is the graveyard of our loved ones and the graveyard of one third of our people.

We came to this wonderful country. We had to overcome many obstacles: new land, new customs, and most of all, a new language. We worked hard, and after many years we had our daughter. We raised our children the best we knew how, and gave them the best we could.

And now, after fifty years, we look around us and we thank G-d for the blessings he bestowed on us. We thank him for our children, Marvin and Eva, Muriel and Scott, and our wonderful grandchildren, Aaron, Jonathan, and little Robie.

No, Hitler did not achieve his goal. He did not completely destroy the Jewish people. Our children and all of your children and grandchildren will carry the torch of Jewishness for generations to come.

And now let us drink "*Le chaim,*" to life and happiness and to all of us, and let us hope and pray that we will be able to celebrate many *simhas* (joyous occasions) together. *Am Israel Chai. (To Israel, life!) Le chaim!*

APPENDIX 2

Muriel's Tribute at the Dedication of Arnold's Plaque

I am sorry that I am unable to be with you as you dedicate this plaque to honor my father's memory. I am with you in spirit.

Those of you who knew my Dad will agree that he was never one to "toot his own horn" and would probably wonder what all the fuss was about. He was truly a gentle man, who never had a bad thing to say about anyone, and he was a wonderful father.

He was also a fighter and a survivor. I mean that in many ways. He was, of course, a Holocaust survivor. When anyone asked him why he survived, he would always say it was luck. And, of course, luck played a part in all survivors' stories. He would never credit his own ingenuity, persistence or spirit of resistance. He would not tell you that he was smuggling in the camps and used his profits to save the life of a woman he barely knew. Nor would he tell you that when he ran out of money, he chose to save her and sacrifice himself. The woman he helped protect became his wife and my mother.

When they came to this country, my parents had nothing but the clothes on their backs. They fought together to made a life for themselves and my brother. My father worked long hours, in miserable conditions, and they survived.

I was born many years later, and the man who was my father was sweet and loving and giving, but it was not until I was older that I saw the real survivor's spirit in him. He suffered from a number of serious chronic health problems in his later years, but he never complained. If asked, he always said he was fine, and then changed the subject. He never gave into his illnesses. He was in the hospital about five years ago, and a cardiologist told him that without a bypass he would not live more than another six months. Then he proceeded to tell him he was not a good candidate for a bypass. I was to be married in a year, but my dad got discharged from the hospital and just kept on living. He danced with me at my wedding, and saw my nephew's *Bar Mitzvah*, and saw my son's *Bris* (circumcision ceremony). We used to joke that he was living on sheer stubbornness.

Even at the very end, my father was a fighter. He had what I am told was a massive coronary, and his heart was already weak, but he kept on fighting. I went to see him in the hospital and I talked to him. He couldn't speak, but he would nod his head. I asked him if he was in pain or needed anything and as was typical, he shook his head, "No." I asked him if he was scared, and he nodded, "No." Then my mother told him he was coming home soon, and again he shook his head, "No." He understood that even a fighter sometimes has to surrender and, bravely, he did so.

Although his fight is over, his spirit survives, and the lessons I learned from him will endure through the generations. Strength can go hand in hand with a quiet, gentle, giving spirit. Thank you for honoring his spirit.

Printed in the United States
48332LVS00005B/169-270

9 781425 920258